Cyphers CC

VICTOR WINSTONE

A brief history of CYPHERS Cricket Club c1890-1990

By the same author

Captain Shakespear
Gertrude Bell
The Illicit Adventure
Leachman 'OC Desert'
Diaries of Parker Pasha
Woolley of Ur
Uncovering the Ancient World
Howard Carter and the discovery of the tomb of Tutankhamun
Royal Copenhagen Porcelain

With Zahra Freeth

Kuwait:Prospect and Reality
Explorers of Arabia

With Gerald de Gaury

Spirit of the East
Road to Kabul

First published in 1998 by
EDWARD GASKELL Publishers
6 Grenville Street
Bideford · Devon
EX39 2EA

ISBN 1 - 898546 - 24 - X

Cyphers CC
A brief history of
CYPHERS Cricket Club
C1890 – 1990

Typeset, printed & bound by
The Lazarus Press
Unit 7 Caddsdown Business Park
Bideford, Devon, EX39 2DX

Dedicated to Cyphers

players past and present

CONTENTS

Introduction

If statistics are to be the measure (and few games have a more apparent susceptibility to tables, aggregates and averages), Cyphers Cricket Club enjoyed its golden era in the aftermath of the Second World War, culminating in the 1950s when, by the standards of the club game in the South of England at any rate, its reputation was unassailable and its achievements, in team and individual terms, exceptional.

Yet there were other periods – for which the statistical evidence is flimsy, most of it having been lost in the turmoil of two wars – when the club's standing might have been even higher. That was in the decades before the outbreak of the First and Second World Wars. As for the earliest period, enough evidence survives in the local press to show that Cyphers men were the equal of WG Grace's famous London County side. As for the 1930s, some of the players who were to contribute to later glories were just taking their places in the club then, vying for selection, travelling mostly by reliable but not always comfortable bus and train services in order to meet up with their motorised seniors at grounds as far removed from their Beckenham base as Streatham and Sutton, Dulwich and Sevenoaks Vine, Beddington and Finchley, usually carrying the bags of seniors who must have been hard task masters and no mean cricketers, and whiting their well–worn 'spikes' on arrival.

In all such matters, facts and figures must await their turn, however, as must the personalities who between them created this small niche in the history of the great game.

Cyphers Cricket Club celebrated its centenary in 1990, but by then it had sacrificed its independence in the battle for financial survival. Among its first fixtures nearly a hundred years earlier were several against a side captained by WG Grace. In the interval, an aristocracy of the game trod its turf – Grace's inseparable friend Murdoch (in the Champion's London County days), Archie Maclaren, the Ashton brothers, Arthur Day, George Beldam the father of cricket photography, HE Enthoven, CTA Wilkinson, Johnny Douglas; and in more recent times, the likes of PBH May, JC Laker, Raman Subba Row, and much of the might of Kent, Surrey and England. It is a history worthy of record, but not for the sake of such names, for they are well remembered in the halls of fame, but for the lesser figures who nonetheless were giants of their own stage and entertainers well able to fill with relish the weekends of suburban enthusiasts and casual sightseers.

As an insignificant playing member of the club, I nonetheless have fond memories of its last two decades of independent existence. Thus, when retirement presented an opportunity to write at leisure and without prior   thought of financial reward, my mind turned to the halcyon days of yore and I decided that I might make myself useful by rescuing surviving records of the club (few as they were) in the hope that I could place on record the ups and downs of a century of cricket in that richly endowed furrow which lies in suburban territory somewhere between South–east London and Kent.

A small question of form. I have stuck throughout to the original spelling of King's Hall Road, so as to avoid jumping on to another horse in mid stream, but realise that nowadays it is Kingshall Road. And while on the subject of writing method, I have been quite inconsistent and unfussed about 'eleven' and 'XI', 'First' and 'Firsts' and '1st', and the various other forms and abbreviations that are the nightmare of all attempts at sports writing.

I must make the traditional declaration that the opinions expressed in this essay, and in particular any errors of date or recollection, are mine alone. All the same, the enterprise has been possible only with the help of a few stalwart survivors, not least Chris Purnell, widow of one of the side's most distinguished post-war captains, Ted Purnell, John Duncan, one of the club's outstanding batsmen in the post Second World War years, and my old friend and occasional skipper Denis Neale, Chairman in the Club's last years, schoolmaster and English expert, who might more profitably have done the job himself. Their help has been indispensable. Help both memorial and documentary also came from old players and the families of members — in particular the Beardwells, Tony Stevens and David Stott, who provided colourful and valuable memories and details. And several old playing members came up with most colourful essays on a favourite subject, the Sussex Tour; to wit, Keith Letchford, David Stott, David Wentworth, Dick Waite and Brian Barnett. Were I to have used all their anecdotes, the book would probably be twice as long, and doubtless twice as amusing. However, economics determine the extent of editorial generosity, and so I have to thank them profusely while condensing their sterling efforts into a page or two. A contribution of undisguised nostalgia came from Rob

Bonnet, and again I wish I could have used more. But of all the cooks who have helped produce this broth, I must single out Roy Wisdom, son of 'Whizz' (no other name will do) whose fame is redoubtable in club and much wider cricket circles. Roy placed at my disposal the wonderful compilation of memorabilia and press comment which his father kept immaculately for some fifty years. Indeed, the three invaluable volumes which mark off Whizz's days from prep school to his retirement, are the basis of the story I have told here, though of course embellished with my own research and, as I have said, with the recollections of others. Without his contribution, the story simply could not have been told.

I thank them all, and gratefully share with them the recollection of summers past when it seems to have rained only rarely, when teas were veritable banquets and the ladies who made and served them angels; of matches in which the most modest of talents blossomed into heroic performance, when dropped catches and injudicious strokes invoked the wrath of captains who alone were allowed to exhibit symptoms of human frailty, but when all trespasses were ultimately forgiven in the golden glow of a jug or two. Happy days!

1

Early Days

In the beginning the name was Brixton Amateurs CC, founded in 1890 by the brothers Charles and Frederick Adye.

The ground was at Dulwich and the first fifteen years were successful enough to warrant a search for new and classier headquarters. Frederick Adye suggested to the committee that a piece of pasture land he owned at Beckenham in Kent might suit; the club could have it at a nominal rent.

And so the freehold of a potentially valuable stretch of Kentish land on what was known as the Cator Park estate was acquired in 1905. Of that piece of manorial estate, WH Ireland's *History of the County of Kent* tells us:

> The parish of Beckenham...is interspersed throughout with handsome seats and buildings, mostly inhabited by persons of fashion and opulence. Its small distance from the metropolis, and pleasant and healthy situation, render it a most desirable retreat from the hurry and bustle of the town...The village [Beckenham] is

situated on the northern side of the parish, having the church, and
Fox grove, near the east end; and a small distance northward is
Beckenham place and park, the house of which only is in the
parish, the out-offices being in that of Bromley. The estate is now
[1830] in the possession of John Cator, esq., standing in the centre
of the park, which is about three miles and a half in circumference,
watered by a branch of the Ravensbourne, the current having been
much widened within the grounds. The present mansion was
erected by John Cator, esq., uncle of the present owner; and the
park occupies portions of the hundreds of Bromley and
Blackheath.[1]

By the time the cricketers from Dulwich arrived on the scene,
Cator Park occupied a favoured place in the developers' all-
embracing eye. And the developer in this rich corner of England's
garden county might have been chosen by Providence to ensure
the permanence of a green patch amid the suburban spread. His
name was John Duncan, director of a local firm of builders of
repute called Syme & Duncan, who in 1885 or 1886 (no one can
be quite certain of the date) had challenged the Cator Estate to a
cricket match on what was then called King's Hall Meadow. After
that, several matches were played and cricket became a familiar
game on the meadow.[2]

Eventually a club was formed in association with the local
church and was given the name Christchurch Institute. In 1902,
that church team moved to a ground on another part of Cator Park
(which it still plays on in the last decade of the 20th century, now

---

[1] WH Ireland, A New and Complete History of the County of Kent, London,
1830, Vol IV, pp616-7.

[2] Present John Duncan to author.

called Stone Park). It was then that the Adyes purchased the freehold from the Cator Estate which, a year or two later, they were pleased to sell on to the Brixton Amateurs.[3]

Looking out from their rich green turf on the developing suburbia that surrounded it, members felt that the club's original name was no longer appropriate. Accepted legend has it that Committee members were unable to agree on a new title and after much debate adopted the neutral and enigmatic Cypher, the Greek letter 'O'. Along with the Cypher went the prancing horse of Kent and the club's adoptive colours, claret, silver and black. Club colours, according to early rule books and fixture lists, could be obtained 'of Messrs. Grieves Ltd., 21 Old Bond Street, London, W.1'.

Thus Cyphers CC came into existence. The date was unquestionably 1904, though 1905 has usually been given as the year in which the new name was officially adopted, and even 1906 has been mooted. The exact date of the first match played on the new ground at King's Hall Road is not known, but it may well have been that WG Grace, then living nearby, was persuaded to lend his august presence to the inaugural game, for on 16th August 1904, the Champion's London County side took the field at King's Hall Road. Cyphers scored 145, WG taking 5 for 57. London County scored 224 for 8, WG scoring 75.

---

[3] Any doubt about the exact date of the club's transition from Brixton Amateurs to Cyphers, is dispelled by a letter from JR Webber, author of the definitive book on WG Grace, 'The Chronicle of WG', giving me details of the first match between his subject's London County XI and Cyphers, citing *The Sportsman*. Details of that and other engagements with London County CC were obtained by Tony Stevens from the *Beckenham Journal. Author*

There is however another, more colourful explanation of so unusual a title as Cyphers, though true patriots might surely think it apocryphal. In a match played on the old ground at Dulwich (in 1906[4], so the story goes) it is alleged that seven of the side were out without scoring, and that in the dressing room after the game they put a brave face on the event by adopting the cypher, the dreaded 'blob', for their new name. It is a version that has been doubted but never effectively contradicted, though the quoted date is certainly in question.

At any rate, it was to Cyphers on the King's Hall Road ground that WG Grace, now living at Crystal Palace and captaining his London County team, brought the first of several sides which sometimes included his Australian friend and rival WL 'Bill' Murdoch. Such men might have been expected to reap a rich harvest against unrenowned club bowling. Surviving records speak well of the club's standard of play, however. WG obviously enjoyed playing on his new neighbour's ground, and he was followed by the likes of Archie MacLaren, Ashtons and Bryans, Stanley Coleman, CTA Williams, the Revd FH Gillingham.

In 1905 an August festival was inaugurated and opponents included Brixton Wanderers, Cheshunt, Enfield and WG Grace's London County CC.

Let the record speak.[5]

---

[4] If it took place at all, it must have been at least two years earlier since the fact that Cyphers were playing at King's Hall Road, or Kent House, in 1904 is in no doubt.

[5] *Beckenham Journal*, July/August 1905 - 1908

'CYPHERS V LONDON COUNTY, played on August 17th (1905) resulting in a win for Cyphers by 33 runs. For the winners, P.S. Snell played an excellent innings for 105, his hits including one six and 12 fours.' In fact, the local press version of events was not quite complete. It seems that after Cyphers' victory in the first innings, a second innings was agreed on by the two captains. Cyphers had scored 44 for 4 when stumps were drawn. The scorecard was probably a little inaccurate too. L. Gale c Woods b Gale should surely read c Woods b Grace. WG took three wickets, not two as the card shows.

CYPHERS

R.H. Jones c Holder		P.S. Snell c Townsend	
bBell...	0	b Grace...	105
E.T. Gale c Woods		E. Bryner b Marshal	7
b Grace...	13	H. Cath lbw bBell...	4
H.E. Smith c Holder		L. Gale c Woods	
b Marshal...	26	b Gale...	4
R.D. Gale c Townsend		A. Smith ht wicket	
b Marshal...	19	b Bell...	15
F. Odell c Holder		H.Gale not out... 6	
b Bell...	2	Extras...	16
		Total	217

LONDON COUNTY

W.G. Grace c L.Gale		G.R.Ryan c Cath b	
b A. Smith...	24	Bryner...	29
C.T.A. Wilkinson		Holder b H.Gale...	31
c&b H. Gale	11	F. Benton c Jones b	
M. Townshend c L.		Bryner..	10

Gale b H.Gale...	0	Rev. H. Williams b	
A. Marshal c&b A.		H. Gale...	0
Smith...	33	B.F. Woods not out...	0
R.M. Bell c L. Gale		Extras...	12
b A.Smith...	16		
Murch b Bryner...	18	Total	184

In those days the club fielded just two elevens, and clearly the Gales and Smiths, along with Snell and Bryner constituted a dominant force.

Cyphers visited the Crystal Palace on 31st May 1906 and on 27th June in the following year.[6]

There was another visit by London County to Kent House in August 1906. The great man's team would fare better this time. Cyphers line up had changed and there were faces that would become familiar over many years on the King's Hall Road ground, including that of LM Simmons who was to captain the club in some of its finest years. The match took place on 2nd August.

The scorecard read:

CYPHERS

W. Pitt b L. de Montezuma...	20
R.H. Jones b L.de Montezuma...	16
H.C. Stembridge c A.N. Other b L. de Montezuma...	3
E.T. Gale c Marshall b L. de Montezuma...	4

---

[6] I have been unable to find a report of either match, and Mr Webber writes 'I have never seen a scorecard for the latter match'. *Author*

L.M. Simmons b W.G. Grace...	13
H. Watson run out...	9
H. Cath hit wicket b W.G. Grace...	18
L. Gale c L.de Montezuma b W.G. Grace...	1
C. Livett st Murch b W.G. Grace...	16
H. Ovenden b L. de Montezuma...	4
H. Gale not out...	0
Extras...	7
Total	111

LONDON COUNTY

P.G. Gale c Stembridge b Pitt...	44
Marshal b Livett...	81
E.H. Jewell b Stembridge...	7
N. Leicester-Clarke c E.T. Gale b Simmons...	35
L. de Montezuma b Simmons...	36
W.G. Grace c Jones b H. Gale...	60
N.A. Damain c Cath b Simmons	14
F.S. Gillespie not out...	29
J.G.L. Smith not out...	42
Extras...	23
Total (for 7 wickets)	371

Sporting Life showed WG with 5 wickets to his name, not 4. But who would argue about a single wicket in such illustrious company?

There was another visit on 1st August 1907. London County scored 259 for 6 decl. (WG 102 not out), Cyphers 178 (WG took 3 wickets).

The details of another game in this panoply of cricket's bygone treasures must be included, the match against Enfield, for the visitors were captained by JWHT Douglas, destined to bring back the Ashes from Australia. PS Snell, who had performed so well for Cyphers against London County, was now playing for the opposition, and Cyphers' no. 11 was club president FJ Adye.

CYPHERS

W. Pitt c Minton b Starkey...	4
R.H. Jones b Minton...	10
H.C. Stembridge lbw b Douglas...	63
E.T. Gale lbw b Starkey...	17
L.M. Simmons b Starkey...	3
H. Cath b Pritchard...	13
H. Gale c Gifford b Starkey...	7
L. Gale c Chard b Starkey...	0
F. Odell b Douglas	6
H. Watson b Douglas...	0
F.J. Adye not out...	5
Extras...	21
Total	189

ENFIELD

J.H. Douglas b H.Gale...	4
J.W.H.T. Douglas b Simmons...	1
R.F. Pritchard c Stembridge b H. Gale...	7
P.S. Snell b Stembridge...	56

A.G.C. Starkey c&b Pitt...   11
W. Chart c Watson b Pitt...   0
A. Minton b Pitt...   0
Chambers b Stembridge...   17
W. Savage b Stembridge...   0
W. Gifford not out   0
W. Pratt b Simmons   9
                              Extras   17
                              Total   122

Finally, Grace's London County came again to King's Hall Road on 28th July, 1908, though the Champion's side had been officially wound up for three years past according to the history books. [7]

LONDON COUNTY

P. Kenward c Pitt b Minton...   1
P.G. Gale b Swain...   50
C.T.A. Wilkinson c Pullen b Pitt...   7
L. de Montezuma b Pullen...   109
W.G. Grace c Swain b Heppell..   23
A. Sims b Pullen...   28
J.D. Gellespie not out...   15
                              Extras...   17
              Total   (for 6 wickets decl)   269

---

[7] In fact, only first-class matches ceased in 1905. The last club game was played on 16th September 1908. *JR Webber to author.*

Carter, F. Benton and C.H. Boyle did not bat

CYPHERS

R.H. Jones b Gillespie...	9
H.G. Swain not out...	175
H.J.E. Stinson c Benton b Gillespie...	20
N. Blake c Benton b Gillespie...	22
W. Pitt c&b Wilkinson...	38
H.C. Stembridge c Kanza b Grace...	15
C.W. Pullen c Wilkinson b Gillespie...	4
H.J. Heppell not out...	0
Extras...	10
Total (for 6 wickets)	<u>293</u>

E.O. Collins, A. Minton, J.H. Radcliffe did not bat.

A tradition of 'good cricket' was soon established and large attendances were common at the new ground which looked out inscrutably on its neighbouring vistas, prosperous Beckenham and Bromley to the north, Crystal Palace of the Great Exhibition and the 'leafy lanes' of Mr Polly's Penge and Anerley to south and west. The motor car was gradually forcing the horse and carriage off the road and esquires and their servants were pulling out of the three-storey houses of the districts. Housemaids and cooks who vacated a myriad attic rooms between Croydon and Brixton and who sought employment elsewhere cast their gaze on nearby suburban housing estates, hurriedly erected by speculative builders for a burgeoning middle class. Most of them looked in vain.

Times had changed, and if things looked grim for the servant class, the new managerial and professional invasion would at least provide a formidable recruiting reservoir for sport and leisure pursuits — for Cyphers, indeed, and its nearby rivals such as Beckenham (founded in 1860) and Bromley, Forest Hill, Dulwich and Catford (Catford was founded in the same year as Cyphers). Club cricket, tennis and bowls in the entire South East seemed to be on the verge of a golden era, though neither promise nor expectation was ever quite realised in the mere two decades which were to lead from the foundation of Cyphers to the onset of the Great War.

Little were the white-clad sportsmen to know as they fought their weekly battles, that in all too brief a time their generation would be engulfed in a less gentlemanly encounter on foreign fields which knew nothing of cricket.

2

Between the wars

Perhaps a retired sports historian with time on his hands will
some day spend a month or two in the newspaper section of
the British Library, or lesser institution, and so unearth a
partial record at least of club cricket in the 1914-18 period when,
as WG Grace insisted, it was not seemly for young men to engage
publicly in sporting activity.

For whatever the great man may have thought of it, we can be
sure that when and where opportunity presented itself, a few
soldiers on leave or men left behind for one reason or another,
banded together for an impromptu game. Most published histories
draw a veil over the period. In any case, few young men survived
the years of carnage, and of those who did few indeed were
physically or mentally ready for sport when peace returned. It was
generally thought that the carefree days of old were gone for ever.
Grace was dead, Hobbs was 35 but with much of his glorious
career to come, and new regimes threatened, though the MCC is

said to have turned down decisively a move to ban that troublesome anachronism the left-handed player from the game.

Frederick Adye and his brother seem not to have been called to active service, though they doubtless served in some way, and were still active when peace came. They saw to it that cricket started up in King's Hall road without delay. By the 1919 season the club was drawing on a few returned servicemen and a new influx of residents, and a modest club house was under construction, no doubt with the participation of the Adyes' building company, and a full-time groundsman was appointed, one Reuben Hicks. In 1920 a tennis section was formed and the same year saw the creation of an outdoor bowling club, the progeny of John Duncan and his partner William Syme[1]. Cyphers was well and truly on the map and a scheme was afoot to raise some £8,000 to purchase the freehold of the ground from the Adyes.

The year 1920 also saw the appearance of the first member of the Beardwell family on Cyphers' turf. Arthur R Beardwell joined the club and came in as a second eleven player, demonstrating that he was a powerful bat and brilliant fielder. He quickly added to the strength of a struggling post-war first eleven and was soon to be followed by two brothers in what proved to be, next to the Duncans, the most enduring of several formidable Cyphers dynasties. Other outstanding players of the 'twenties were WA and FJ Wardle, wicket keeper 'Jimmy' Radcliffe, H Cath who had played against Grace's team in the first decade of the century,

---

[1] The present John Duncan, note to author 22nd Oct 1997. The William Syme Trophy and William Syme's Cup became two of the best known prizes in the sport.

bowlers WW Pullen and LM Simmons who had captained the side since pre-war days, Rupert Holloway, WR Beardwell, PB Wise and NP Andrews, Phillips and another keeper, Hallows, one of whose relatives played for Lancashire and England. But the club's star batsman at the time was undoubtedly WLT 'Tag' Webb, a prodigal scorer who once made four centuries in Cricket Week against visitors who included strong MCC and Kent Club and Ground elevens.

Of the few surviving records of the time, photographs and press reports record one of the most damaging rain storms ever to hit the district. On Thursday May 26th, 1922, between 2pm and 3.15pm, Beckenham was subjected to widespread storms which left the entire neighbourhood, including Cyphers' small pavilion and ground under water. The called it the 'Great Storm'.

As for the club itself, a membership card for 1927 preserved in the Beardwell family gives us the names of officials, as well as early fixture lists. President was FH Oliver and the list of vice-presidents read: CW Adye, FJ Adye, A Andrews, T Andrews, FW Barber, EW Belleini, FG Billett, EA Foss, CM Gibson, FW Lovell, H Perkins, FJ Winner. The club committee consisted of LM Simmons, EW Belleini, Rupert Holloway, FP Hodes, HJ Parsons, JS Douglas, FW Winser, JC Poole, FJ Doggett, FJ Adye, J Cullum, and WS Knight. Hodes was Hon Sec. Captains of cricket were: First XI, LM Simmons (vice R Holloway); Second XI, EW Belleini (HM Patterson); Third XI, EA Chapman (JD Smith); Fourth XI, RS Johnstone (EW Pettman). The cricket committee: FJ Adye, WR Beardwell, GW Clement, RD Gale, HA Gibson, EK McKay.

The First XI fixture list had been established soon after the war and was to remain substantially unchanged throughout the club's years of independent existence: Beckenham, traditionally the season's opener, followed by Sutton, Kent C&G, Private Banks, Ibis, Surbiton, Westminster Bank, Kenley, Gravesend, Forest Hill, Lloyds Bank, MCC, Wanderers, Harrow, Dulwich, Barclays Bank, Sutton, NP Bank, Lloyds, Beddington, with of course the return fixtures. Coutts Bank was also a regular appointment at that time and South Hampstead Bexley and Wallington featured in the lists of lower elevens.

Success bred success, and it was decided that the club should be constituted as a limited liability company and shares sold to the value of £8,000. Of course, the shares could only be disposed of to club members or their close relatives, otherwise ownership and control would soon find their way into unsympathetic and perhaps antagonistic hands. The shareholders would form a new company which would, of course, own the very valuable freehold property acquired from the Adyes. As it happened, only 5,000 one-pound shares were sold. A few of the more affluent members consequently took up the remaining 3,000 shares and a private company, King's Hall Sports Ground Ltd, was formed. That body granted a lease to Cyphers Club.[2] As before, the club would pay all current running expenses and assume responsibility for the maintenance and use of the ground and its associated buildings. What could be more sensible or mutually beneficial? The shareholders' investment was protected for all time – short of some unforeseen catastrophe – by the intrinsic value of the site, and the club was in possession of a playing area of immense potential in a wealthy and developing suburban area that could

---

[2] Stevens, A., *Catford Cyphers Cricket Club*, Centenary publication, 1990.

reasonably be expected to provide members and players of the required skill and social acceptability into the distant future.

For more than fifty years, that early expectation proved justified. In its train it brought decades of high-grade cricket and tennis against the best opposition in the South of England, to say nothing of an international reputation for open air and indoor bowls. Events as yet unsuspected and unpredictable would show that the agreement contained the seeds of disenchantment. But as the 1930s approached there were no such forebodings. All was for the best in that best of all possible worlds.

Cyphers was not alone in sensing the new expansive quality of life in its neighbourhood. The Beckenham Club, for example, just to the south in Foxgrove Road, was a thriving centre of cricket and tennis with first-class playing and social facilities for members and visitors. Between these two leading Beckenham clubs, off Lennard and Copers Cope roads, vast areas of lush pasture had become (or were in the process of becoming) the manicured sportsfields of the great banks — Lloyds, Midland, Westminster (NatWest); and only a little further afield, Britannic House (BP).

õ

In keeping with its growing status, and the nature of the opposition, Cyphers began to see the need for a new clubhouse and pavilion. Theirs must be patently as grand as any in the South East, and by chance the man who could help to make it possible had established his position in the club as a resolute middle order bat. He was also a successful builder whose firm, Holloway Bros., were major contractors in the construction of the new Bank of England in Threadneedle Street.

Money for the proposed new clubhouse came from donations, loans and surplus cash.[3] But it would be another six years or more before it came to fruition. Support came too from the Tulse Hill Hockey Club which hired the ground during its season.

Gradual if unspectacular progress through the 'twenties had given rise to a steady swell of talent and strength in all the club's sections, not least cricket. Surviving annual reports give at least an outline impression of Cyphers CC in action as the 'thirties came into focus.

By 1930, the position of the first eleven in terms of South of England club cricket was fairly reflected in the year's statistics — 103 matches played, 24 won, 40 lost, 39 drawn. The side was still skippered by LM Simmons, a class bowler and good all-rounder of much presence on and off the field. WA Wardle, the club's mainstay, had an aggregate of 830 runs and headed both batting and bowling averages. Six first eleven batsmen ended the season (the first for which complete records have survived) with averages in the twenties. They were WA Wardle, GP Parker, KFP Downing, PB Wise, LM Simmons, and R Holloway. That five of these players also headed the equally modest bowling figures (averaging from 19.85 to 25.02 per wicket), is indicative of all-round capability at the top but also of a distinct need for some improved individual performances and for playing reinforcement. The first eleven attack at that time depended heavily on the fast-medium pace of AWR Matthews and the senior all-rounder Wardle, and there was much lamenting of the absence of a reliable spinner. By

---

[3] ibid.

1930, Arthur Beardwell was captain of the 2nd XI, supported by his brother Albert (AE). The other playing member of the dynasty, Walter R, ended the season with 358 runs from 25 innings for the Firsts.

The following season produced much the same mixed bag of statistics, though one of the senior players, GP Parker, had a batting average of 35.00 from only six innings, while WR Beardwell managed just over 28, JA Bills 24.67 from twenty innings; the rest of the seniors trailed below the 20 mark.

It was the achievements of some of the newer and younger 2nd eleven players that gave rise to most optimism. WR Burrough, with 13 innings and a best score of 101, topped the averages with 32.17. And an 18 year old who had shown promise as a schoolboy at Dulwich, EM Wisdom, made an initial appearance as a left hander with an aggregate score of 174 from nine matches (twice not out), an average of just under 25. Known to all as 'Whizz', (spelt indifferently with one 'z' and two) he, Burrough and other youngsters paid their one guinea subscription, having convinced the committee that they were of acceptable social and playing promise, and were duly admitted to membership. Whizz produced an *Alleynian* magazine report from his last year at Dulwich College, which said 'Good fast left handed bowler: works very hard and keeps a good length. Very useful hitter'. At his prep school, Abbey, he had shone as a bat but at Dulwich, where cricket coach was the Kent bowler Marriott, he batted low in the order and often opened the bowling. He went into the 3rd eleven at Cyphers but was clearly cut out for higher things. Other young members were challenging for First XI places, too. By now the club boasted four Saturday elevens.

Next year, 1932, was much like its predecessor in terms of overall performance, but some of the players who would dominate the club in future years were making expected progress at higher levels, notably Burrough and Wisdom, both as bats, though both had considered bowling to be their chief claim to recognition when they left school. 1931 showed more progress, particularly in batting where eight players scored the coveted century (with Tadman's 133n.o. the highest of the season). 1932 gave rise to something approaching euphoria in the Cricket Section. Of 95 matches played, 39 were won, 33 lost and 23 drawn. At last the club could count more victories than defeats at the end of the season. WA Wardle headed the 1st eleven batting and was third in the bowling figures, while another brother, JP, headed the 2nd eleven batting and was fourth in the bowling table. Even better results were forecast by the elders in their annual report.

Indeed, the Committee's report for the 1933 season began with the words – 'The expectation expressed a year ago of a successful season for 1933 has been fulfilled in no small measure. The first eleven in particular have justified our optimism, winning more matches than in any year since the war.' Out of 98 matches played, 44 were won, 30 lost, and 23 drawn; one was tied. To quote the Committee report again: 'The batting was generally more consistent than for the past few years while the bowling and fielding showed a distinct improvement'.

Webb, who had suffered a setback in batting form the year before, returned to his expected level of performance and headed the first eleven averages at 34.00, with a highest score of 108 not out against Kenley. By now the three Beardwells were distributed through the first, second and third elevens, AE, WR and AR. It was the latter who topped the club's batting table for the year with 695 runs from 22 innings (4 times not out) at an average of 38.61. Scores of 110 against Beddington, 91 not against Nat Prov and 56 against Dulwich, suggested that there might yet be peaks waiting to be climbed. It was another third eleven player, RE Court, who won the Committee's praise for the innings of the year, with 160 n.o. against Spencer III. The veteran WA Wardle achieved the best batting aggregate, 746 runs for the first XI (2nd in the averages at 32.43), and also topped the bowling with 62 wickets at 16.5 apiece.

It was the young Whizz's first full year in the first eleven. In the July Cricket Week he distinguished himself with a top score of 63 against Kent Club and Ground; in fact, he was the highest scorer by far on either side in a low scoring game. Again, he was said by his superiors to have shown promise if not actual achievement.

õ

The home and away games against Sutton were always high on the list of needle matches. In 1933, the London *Evening Standard* sent its club cricket reporter along. In the leisurely style of the day he wrote:

> I spent a few hours at Sutton on Saturday, and for the second time this season they were beaten. Cyphers were their masters, but it has to be said that until next month the Cheam-road club will not be at full strength. Full credit must be given to Cyphers for their win, for their bowling, particularly that of W.A. Wardle and K.S.B. Downing, found the weak spots in the home batting. The former got a lot of runs last summer for the Cyphers, as also did J.P. Wardle his brother. W.A. Wardle bowls a slow ball, and

Downing, whom I do not remember having seen before as a
bowler, is pretty fast. He showed that his batting is as good as ever
for he was the leading scorer in the match with 49.

The *Morning Post* reported on 'Cyphers' Week', declaring it an
'enjoyable' festival 'without fully representative sides'. Victory
over Gravesend, with a fifth-wicket stand between Wardle (89)
and Bills (50), was described as the week's highlight:

'Cyphers' batting broke down against the M.C.C., A.E.
Beardwell's 44 being top score, and they lost by six wickets', said
the paper. It praised Wisdom's innings against Kent C&G. 'Having
scored ten runs Cyphers were held up by the rain, and when play
was resumed they had only an hour in which to make 100 runs.
E.M.Wisdom attacked the bowling in great style and in forty
minutes rattled up 63 runs by means of two 6's and nine 4's, with
the result that Cyphers gained a thoroughly deserved win by four
wickets just before time.' [4]

It is perhaps worth glancing at the 1933 season's leading batting
figures for the purpose of later comparison, if for no other:

	inns	n.o.	runs	highest score	ave
WLT Webb	18	2	544	108*	34.00
WA Wardle	24	1	746	89	32.43
KFP Downing	20	1	587	125	30.89
TW Boyd	10	5	145	76*	29.00
JA Bills	19	6	332	73	25.54
R Holloway	17	5	275	63	22.92
EM Wisdom	19	1	204	47	17.00

---

[4] *Morning Post*, July 18, 1933

What, then, was the Saturday scene like at this time, as King's Hall Road settled to the familiar picture of men in white and the disturbance of the peace by loud choruses of appeal?

Certainly the club had become an accepted part of the social and sporting life of Beckenham and its surroundings. Crowds often gathered on the embankment which reached gently along the north-west corner of the ground, from King's Hall Road towards the lawn tennis courts. Some of the club's star performers like openers Parker and Bills, the all-rounders Wardle and Matthews, the Beardwells with their hard hitting and brilliant close fielding, attracted personal followings.

But the general picture could hardly have been better portrayed than by a letter from Australia published in the *Beckenham Journal* on Saturday 4 March, 1933. It was headed 'Cricket Down Under' and began by explaining that the author, Mr Walter Brain of Lewisham, NS Wales, was inspired to write by the Ashes test series then in progress in Australia. He concluded:

For several years, during and since the War, I was resident in England, and during the summer months when cricket was on, used to go on Saturdays down to the 'Cyphers' ground at New Beckenham, where I saw cricket being played under ideal conditions according to my way of thinking...I can see it all now in my mind's eye, as I lounged on the grassy bank near the road – the pretty pavilion with the background of trees opposite to me, the green turf and the quiet enjoyment of watching high class cricket being played for the game's sake alone. I have seen the game played at Lords, the Oval and the Australian grounds, but I have never enjoyed a day's cricket as I did those spent on the ground of the 'Cyphers' at New Beckenham, and through your columns I hope I would like to thank the gentlemen who comprise the teams... for the many happy hours which I spent while in England watching them play.

The following year was marked by the appearance of an experienced and outstanding opener at King's Hall Road, TH Jenner. Unfortunately, the strength he imparted was offset by the loss of form of some of the other seniors, with another disappointing season resulting. Fielding was consistently pinpointed as the weakest aspect of the club's play at this time, though one or two players like Rupert Holloway, in almost any position in the field, and AE Beardwell at first slip, were outstanding.

Jenner, a teacher at Oakfield School, Penge, had been earning his living in Liverpool since 1928, where he played League cricket for Sefton Park, along with another player who came south to Cyphers, JS Mason. He had at least one memorable trait in the field. He always threw in from behind his back, an awkward looking action but one that produced great accuracy of aim. Jenner's rise to the top of the batting averages in his first year, with a figure marginally under 30, was no more than observers of his excellent technique expected; neither were Wardle's second places in both the batting and bowling figures.

A new groundsman, George Wager, appeared in 1933, taking over from Hicks who was persuade to leave the job and become the personal servant of old FJ Adye, the club's founder and benefactor. Hicks, whose brother Alfred was a foreman at Syme and Duncan for more than thirty years, returned to Beckenham a few years later, on Mr Adye's death, to become groundsman at the

Beckenham Technical College. He was to umpire for the club for many years[5].

õ

Though not in itself a year of notable achievement, 1935 nonetheless came to display some hoped for plumage. Wisdom, ever 'Whizz', never Egerton, the name he was given at birth, or Eric which he admitted to and preferred, made the transition from promising and at times brilliant youngster to prolific adult. He passed the personal mark of 2,000 runs for the season, more than half of them for representative sides for which, increasingly, he was asked to play. Though in his early twenties still, he was already a much respected – not to say feared – batsman in senior club circles. At school, where his seam bowling seems to have attracted most attention, his batting was described simply as 'unorthodox'. He was an unmistakable figure at the wicket, square of build, with strong forearms and lightning reactions. He always gave the bowler exaggerated hope by taking leg-stump guard and assuming a front-on position several inches outside his mark. Naturally enough the bowler took a full view of the stumps as an invitation to knock them over and usually concentrated on middle and off, only to find his first ball disappear for four or six, through or over extra cover. Having announced his intentions early on he would, as often as not, amass a century or more by early afternoon while other more orthodox colleagues assessed the bowling circumspectly and not uncommonly came to grief. In

---

[5] John Duncan to author, *ibid.*

1934, though having to fight for a middle order place in Cyphers' batting line up, he had been offered membership of the highly selective Stoics, and played his first game for them in June 1935, going in at number five against a strong Incognito XI (which incidentally included EW Swanton at number 3) at the Oval. He scored 19 and took one catch in a match that was lost by three wickets. Another Cyphers player, wicket-keeper EMG Austin, was also a regular Stoic at this time.

By 1935, Whizz topped the first eleven averages at 35.33, made the highest individual score of 126 against Ibis, and the largest aggregate, 905 from 25 completed innings. He also, as much to his own surprise as anyone's, took four wickets against Beddington, including the openers Winter and Birkett and number 3 Johnson. EA Grant[6], the excellent scorer for the Firsts with an irrepressible penchant for versifying, was so impressed that he wrote a ditty to commemorate the feat, the first verse of which ran:

> Four wickets in a single match,
> Four wickets in a day,
> No wonder that our scorer's dumb
> It takes your breath away.

It was, in a sense, the year of the formal introduction of one of the finest club batsmen of the period to a stage that he would dominate in years to come.

There was another achievement worthy of comment in 1935. EA Griffin, a regular third eleven bowler who sometimes turned his arm for the seconds, took 97 wickets at an average of 13.1, the

---

[6] Grant became First XI scorer soon after the First World War. Duncan *ibid.*

highest number of wickets taken by a Cyphers bowler in a single season to that date. It was a poor season for the club all the same, with a total 33 victories from 96 matches by the four elevens, with 38 lost, 24 drawn and one tied. Defeats at the hands of MCC, Kent C&G and the Wanderers in Cricket Week, and old enemies like Beckenham, Sutton and Westminster Bank in Saturday fixtures, were only partly compensated by wins against Gravesend, Ibis and Sutton. Poor fielding, some good performances by younger members in the lower elevens, and the news the Beckenham Council had approved plans for the new pavilion after five years of debate, architectural scheming and fund raising, gave the year the variegated appeal of the curate's egg. Play was relegated to the back pitch for the start of the 1936 season. Everything gave way to the building project that was to mark Cyphers' place on cricket's map for ever and a day.

On 30th May, 1936, the new pavilion was officially opened by Sir Edward T. Campbell, MP for Bromley and a versatile sportsman. Before the evening's speeches and celebrations, he turned out for the club against visitors Surbiton. In a rain affected match he was robbed of a knock at number 7, but bowled effectively, taking two wickets. Jenner was 66 n.o. in Cyphers' score of 133 for 3 at the close. The match was abandoned as a draw, and rain caused the opening festivities to be held in the hall and under the long balcony of the pavilion.

'...with the completion of this magnificent building, the most cherished hopes and ambitions of those who have worked for the

Club for so many years, have been realised.' So wrote the *Beckenham Journal*[7]. Edward Campbell spoke characteristically of 'team spirit', of his own devotion to cricket, and he thought it a pity that the new generation paid so much attention to 'lesser games', to the detriment of the 'great game'. The response of the tennis section is not recorded. A year later, as if to stress the club's variety of allegiances, an indoor bowls clubhouse was opened and was soon the scene of national and international engagements. Many were the visitors, even county and test players, who would in later years express surprise and envy when they came upon Cyphers' pavilion with its capacious bar, its long exterior balcony, its changing rooms, bathing and shower facilities, bar steward's living quarters. Only the wealthiest clubs of whatever status could begin to compare with it in size, grandeur and amenity.

The year of the Pavilion was also the year of a change of leadership. Simmons, a stern and much respected skipper, decided to hand over to his vice-captain Rupert Holloway and was immediately offered the Chairmanship of the club. Now the head of a successful building firm, Holloway was the ideal man to assume the captaincy of a side that he had played in since 1919. Before the First World War he played both football and cricket for Townley Park, a club based on Townley Road, Dulwich, and he became an English soccer international. It was he who introduced Matthews to Cyphers as a young cricketer and it was the latter who, when Townley Park was eventually disbanded, talked his old mentor into joining him at King's Hall Road. The side he now

---

[7] *Beckenham Journal*, Saturday, June 6, 1936

captained was on paper one of the strongest clubs in London and the Home Counties. Its main opposition was getting stronger too.

One performance stood out from all others in the 1936 season. The *Evening Standard* tells the tale:

> E.M Wisdom, the Cyphers CC. batsman to whose six-hitting feats I have previously referred, set up a new club record this week-end. Cyphers were left by Forest Hill to get 150 in some 95 minutes, and lost two wickets cheaply. Then Wisdom hit 73 in 24 minutes, the fastest scoring ever recorded on the ground. His first 50 included two sixes and nine fours...

Scorer Grant next day sent 'Whizzy' a note. 'I thought you should have a copy of your scoring in yesterday's match. Time 5.54: 4,4,4,4,2,1,4,1,3,4,1,1,1,1,4,4,4,4,6,6,1,2,2,1,4 6.18: St CS Taylor b.Dean - 73.' Several stanzas of verse were included.

As the Committee's laconic report for the next year put it, '1937 passed quietly into the Club's history'. In one respect, this was a momentous time for all cricketers. The 1936-7 season had seen the general introduction of the new lbw law which, for the first time, allowed an appeal for a ball which pitched outside the stumps, so long as the batsman's pad was in front of the wicket at the moment of impact. But only a ball pitching outside the off stump was eligible. Bradman, just approaching his imperious best, looked forward to the ball pitching outside the leg stump being allowed, and he even advocated that it should not be necessary for the batsman's leg to be between wickets if, in the umpire's view, it would have hit the wicket. As many a lesser cricketer observed when he heard Bradman's view, 'It's all right for him'.

The gloomy report of the committee at the season's end wasn't always reflected in score-sheets or the press. In fact, the 1937 season at Cyphers began with a batting discovery which promised much only to deceive. The long awaited partner for opener Jenner turned up in the shape of HA Southgate. A powerful bat with good technique, he came with a reputation ready made at Bedford CC, and in Minor Counties appearances. He soon proved his worth at King's Hall Road. But by the end of June he was called away to Portsmouth for 'business reasons' never to be seen again. The magnitude of the loss can be judged from the fact that in his brief stay with the club he made 303 runs at an average of 43.29. The achievement of the year none the less was the amazing feat of bowler AWR Matthews who took all ten wickets against Sutton for 36 runs.

The highlight for the growing army of club supporters, all the same, was the start of the season fixture against Beckenham. So popular had this annual battle become that the national Sunday newspapers placarded it locally and at rail stations along the Beckenham-London line, and sent their star sports reporters to Foxgrove Road or King's Hall Road. They weren't disappointed in May 1937. Jenner and Southgate put on 155 for the first wicket and Cyphers declared at 260 for two. Beckenham were despatched for 147, Margham taking 4 for 39.

At the end of June came the popular Left-handers versus Right-handers annual fixture in which, Alice like, the left-handers batted right handed and vice versa, played as the _Cricketer_[8] recalled on the 'charming Addiscombe ground' in aid of Croydon General Hospital. Whizz was the only Cypher on that occasion. And in September, a Kent XI was entertained at Foxgrove Road by a combined Cyphers and Beckenham team for Leslie Ames's

---

[8] _The Cricketer_, 26 June 1937

benefit. The hosts scored 185 for 7; Kent replied with 187 for 3, Frank Woolley coming in at number four and finishing with a breezy 72, before he was caught by Pickering of Beckenham off Matthews' bowling. Stoics CC contributed to the off-field joys of the year with a 60th anniversary dinner at Frascatis on 29th October. Cyphers was represented by its President, Beckenham Councillor FP Hodes, and the two regular Cyphers members of the side. And there was the annual supper of the infamous 'Bootleggers' at the Cheshire Cheese, one of Whizz's favourite charity sideshows. An annual Bootlegger's tour to Holland each June, to play against De Flamingo's at the Hague and enjoy that club's magnificent hospitality at the Dutch equivalent of Lord's, was a mandatory entry in the Wisdom diary.

There were four thriving Cyphers elevens turning out every Saturday at this time; but gaps in batting and bowling strength marked the annual, anguished cries of the committee.

Summer smiled magnificently on 1938's cricket. Early on in May, the Sunday paper *Reynolds News*[9] captured the spirit of the moment with the headline on its main sports page, 'Cyphers had Wisdom, but bid fails'. It referred to the club's first match against Bromley, a new and competitive fixture which ended in a draw after Cyphers, chasing 250, more or less gave up the pursuit when Whizz carelessly ran himself out for the highest score of the day, 87. The 'notable performances' section of the annual report

---

[9] *Reynolds News*, 22 May 1938

showed that keeper EMG Austin, who headed the averages for the year, recorded 120n.o. against Westminster Bank and 52 against Gravesend, while taking as ever a good bag behind the stumps; Wisdom scored 103 against Sutton, and 98n.o. against Hornsey, as well as the 87 against Bromley; WH Humphreys notched up 108n.o. against Kent Club and Ground in Cricket Week, 50 against Stoics and 79 against Lloyds Bank; another recent recruit PHS Wadham took 93 off the Surbiton bowling, while the irrepressible TH Jenner failed remarkably to score a century in the season but accumulated 83 and 68 not out in the two Gravesend matches. Tinsley and Simmons were the backbone of the bowling, sending down 736 and 725 overs respectively at 22 and 23 per wicket. Simmons's 7 for 82 against Beddington was probably the bowling highlight of the season. But club match figures of 98 played, 30 won, 43 lost 25 drawn speak for themselves. The Thirds, skippered by FA Jenkins, showed up the best in an undistinguished honours list.

In Cricket Week 1938, a young wicket-keeper batsman by the name of Evans was top scorer for Kent Club and Ground. Going in at number 6, he scored 105. More would be heard of him after a hiatus of some seven years. But the year would be remembered chiefly for the retirement of one of the greatest of all Kent and England cricketers, Frank Woolley, for the headlines in August that announced '903 for 7 declared, Australia 19 for 2 — Hutton 364'; headlines shared with the shooting down of a Chinese aircraft by twelve Japanese fighter planes, a bellicose speech by Herr von Ribbentrop Germany's ambassador to the Court of St James, the serialisation in the *Evening News* of a new novel called 'Brighton Rock', and the defeat of Holland's Flamingos on their annual visit to England by a Cyphers side playing its first ever Sunday game at King's Hall Road. It was a convenient if not exactly auspicious time for Whizz, Cyphers most distinguished run maker, described in the press as the 'well-known Beckenham cricketer', to marry. He took Miss Meriel Jackson to the altar of St Matthew's church, Croydon, at the end of November, as the clouds of war gathered.

õ

The reader must take account of the fact that 1939's committee report was written at the end of a season which seemed to be specially capable of spawning false hopes. Expectations of a climb down by the Axis powers were quickly dashed, though there were at that time thoughts of gentlemanly conduct on the battlefields. But by the winter months when the club captain Rupert Holloway put in his report to the Committee, there was certainly no hint of panic, nationally or in King's Hall Road. The Committee might, indeed, be accused of complacency, even of a lack of patriotism, had they not already in the course of half a century demonstrated their mastery of understatement. To them, dropped catches remained the issue of the moment, far, far more important than dropped bombs; the mistakes of captaincy much more deplorable than maladroit military leadership. To quote the opening of the report:

> It was a profound disappointment to all Members that, owing to the outbreak of war, the season was abruptly ended when a full month's fixtures remained to be played.

Not to be held back by a mere declaration of war, the Committee went on to make it plain that it was not entirely happy about a year in which, of 80 matches played only 21 were won, while 28 were lost and 31 left drawn. Apart from the customary depredations of the weather, the 4th eleven lost two fixtures because opponents were engaged in Territorial activities.

A story that has come down from 1938 must be included in any story of cricket of whatever calibre. The Fourth eleven were short of a player in their game against NP Bank and to make up their number they talked a tennis player who had never held a cricket bat in anger to join them. His name was Russell Rudd. He was a strong tennis player with a sharp eye for a ball and he went in to bat on the back pitch at an unremarkable moment on the Saturday afternoon in question. An hour and a half later he had scored 202 not out and his captain declared. Never, it is said, was such mayhem seen on the wicket which overlooked the rear gardens of King's Hall Road. It was in the previous year, 1937 that AWR Matthews, one of the most devastating opening bowlers in the club's history and a fine bat withal, took all ten wickets against Sutton for 36 runs, every one of them clean bowled. That was the period, too, of some of the great achievements of another fast bowler and all-rounder, RH Ames, nephew of the great Leslie Ames of Kent. In 1938 he was second behind Wardle in the bowling figures, with 5 for 36 against the touring Dutchmen, the Flamingos. He made innumerable good scores in the middle order batting but seldom bothered to stay for his centuries.

In such company it is hard to think in terms of 'exceptional' talent, yet the last season of peace saw a potentially remarkable addition to the club's strength with the appearance of TC Johnston, a player whose provenance cannot be traced with any certainty in the records but who came immediately from the Somerset Stragglers. He joined sometime after the start of the 1939 season, and went in to bat at number four for the First XI. On 20th May, the *Beckenham Journal* reported the previous Saturday's game against Sutton and observed, 'The Cyphers have found a very useful man in TC Johnstone (sic) who bowled and batted well'. Ten days later, the *Evening Standard* wrote: 'Cyphers new player, T.C. Johnston from Somerset Stragglers, played a large part in their defeat of Bickley Park, for besides hitting up 118 in only 93 minutes, he also took three wickets for 19. Johnston hit three sixes and 15 fours, and with W.R Burrough, also batting stylishly for 87, Cyphers declared at 295 for seven. As Johnston scored another century yesterday against Westminster Bank, his worth to Cyphers can be appreciated'. In fact, he made 133 against Westminster Bank. There followed scores of 80n.o. against the Dutch tourists, 78 v Stoics, 71 Lloyds Bank, 56 Gravesend, etc, etc, heading the batting averages for the year at 55.98 from 14 innings, a figure that had never before been achieved at Cyphers. Not content with that, he opened the bowling and proceeded to top the figures in that department with 35 wickets at 17 runs apiece. He would enjoy one more intermittent season with the club.

Another opener, JS Standerwick, had joined Jenner at the end of the 1938 season and he was succeeded by Frank Copeland who graced the 1939 season with stylish batting and some profitable partnerships.

Once again, the dry statistics for the years 1938 and 1939 make interesting reading, showing how the example of one strong player can lead to all-round improvement.

1938

	ings	n.o.	runs	highest score	ave
EMG Austin	25	7	492	120*	27.33
TH Jenner	20	1	473	83	24.89
JA Standerwick	10	-	247	50	24.70
R Holloway	19	8	265	37	24.09
WA Wardle	7	2	120	46	24.00
F Copeland	21	-	467	62	22.24
EM Wisdom	27	1	569	103	21.89
PHS Wadham	27	2	521	93	21.84

Wardle headed the bowling figures with an average of 16.9.

1939

	ings	n.o.	runs	highest score	ave
TC Johnston	14	1	727	135	55.98
TH Jenner	18	1	789	122	46.41
EM Wisdom	21	4	667	87*	39.25
JA Bills	23	5	207	55*	25.87
F Copeland	17	-	435	66	25.58
R Holloway	17	3	261	38	18.64

Then the bowling figures for 1939:

	overs	maidens	runs	wcks	ave
TC Johnston	154.2	20	595	35	17.00
WA Wardle	140.3	5	808	39	20.72
CH Tinsley	139.2	8	706	26	27.15
PHS Wadham	154.4	16	691	25	27.64

The perceptive reader may notice that the omnipresent name Wardle had been absent from the records for two years. The prodigal all-rounder had fallen victim to the social snobbery of his day. He had suffered a number of business misfortunes and in 1936 was in need of a job and a roof over his head. The new pavilion came, he thought, as a gift from heaven, with its built-in flatlet for a bar manager. But when he mentioned the idea to the Committee they would have none of it. Members and servants and all that. Wardle went off in high dudgeon but returned in 1938 after making his reluctant protest.

'Whizz' and AE Beardwell were the highest aggregate run makers in 1939, and Jenner was not far behind them. But if he had batted for a full season. It is an appropriate note on which to leave behind the halcyon days of the 'Thirties; the last decade of that between-the-wars period when the ageing Bradman and the young Hutton reigned at the highest level, when Indian nobles still played their cricket for England, Pakistan was unheard of, and the West Indies were not yet a serious force in the world; when clubs such as Cyphers were the preserve of 'gentlemen', with all their transparent faults and rough hewn virtues.

3

War and Peace

'It will not be out of place to record here that the following
members of the Cricket Section, some of whom were able to play
in the early part of the season, are now serving in H.M.Forces:
*Messrs Eric Austin, R.H.Ames, P.E.Bavister, R.A.Black,
L.W.Black, J.Bonham, R.J.S.Booty, L.H.Baker, D.N.Court,
E.Connelly, P.A.Chappell, T.W.French, H.A.Goff, B.H.Holloway,
T.C.Johnston, J.C.Lynn, D.McCall, K.W.Philp, J.R.Richardson,
F.W.Rodgers, G.P.Thompson, H.J.Tomkins, P.H.S.Wadham,
H.A.M.Whyte, S.R.Wiltshear.'*

So wrote the acting assistant hon. secretary of the section at
the end of the 1940 season. To meet the demands of the
national emergency, with players disappearing at a
moment's notice, it was decided to field only two regular sides on
Saturdays, nominated 'A' and 'B'. Nevertheless, in the early part
of the season it proved possible to raise an irregular 3rd eleven.

As in the year before, individual achievement failed to generate team success. There was a full fixture list with 20 matches. All-rounder Johnston, in the nine innings before his enlistment, made enough runs and took enough wickets to occupy second place in the season's batting averages (50.86), and first place among the bowlers (15.09). He made two centuries, his highest score being 114 against Private Banks, and took four wickets for 40 against Sutton. Jenner headed the batting figures with 50 or more in nine successive matches, four of which scores were centuries, averaging 55.72. His top score of 141 was made against Sutton. Whizz, as was expected, made a major contribution to the batting, exceeding 50 five times out of nine, once against Sutton when he made 50 in 12 minutes, 57 in 20 minutes, in partnership with Johnston (46 n.o.). Behind Jenner (who had also become an accomplished if reluctant wicket-keeper) and Johnston, came the familiar names of WA Wardle, CH Tinsley and F Copeland. A much needed regular wicket keeper, WE Phillips, came to the rescue of the 'A' eleven. He was said to be especially good on the leg side, and claimed five stumpings and eight catches in the season. Skipper Rupert Holloway kept up his fielding reputation with eight catches. It wouldn't do, however, to paint a one-side picture of Cyphers' performance at this time. In a not very successful season overall there was one dismal collapse. In June 1940, chasing Beddington's 200 for 8 declared, Cyphers were all out for 56. The Beddington bowler GW Morris claimed six for 26.

The 'B' team, led by Fred Jenkins, played 19 matches, winning four, losing eleven and drawing three, with one tied result. The Beardwell brothers had become the backbone of the Bs, though each was more than capable of helping out in the senior side when asked. AR (Arthur) ended the season with an average of 30.18, AE

(Albert) with 25.55 and WR with 24.14. It was another member of the old brigade, EA Griffin, who bore the brunt of the bowling, however, sending down 165 overs and claiming 36 wickets at a cost of 21.13 each. A newly joined youngster, NP Reeves, promised much for the immediate future. A medium-fast bowler with a cultured action, he joined towards the end of the season and took 15 wickets from 42 overs, thus heading the averages at 11.13. Against NatProv he took 8 for 29.

George Wager, the groundsman who had given the club yeoman service since taking over from 'Reg' Hicks in 1933, became a critical servant during the early part of the war, when call-up papers took both members and staff at a moment's notice. He had to prepare two wickets each week-end under all kinds of difficulty, not least the dropping of enemy bombs, mines and incendiary devices. The Committee was anxious to express its gratitude, as it would be for many a year to come.

The last two Saturday fixtures in September were cancelled because of enemy action. The blitz had begun in earnest.

Opponents fell away as war increasingly dictated the terms by which leisure activities were pursued. But in 1941, a summer made sizzling by nature and spectacular by the enemy saw to it that a full fixture list was completed between the first Saturday of May and the third Saturday of September. So inviting were the early days of autumn, indeed, that two extra fixtures were squeezed in on the last Saturday of September and the 'A' eleven enjoyed extra matches on the first two Saturdays of October. Truly the war was an irritation to those who were left behind to keep the flag of club cricket flying; but it can hardly be said to have dominated the thinking of men like Rupert Holloway and Tom Jenner, captain and vice, since the retirement of Simmons just before the outbreak of war. In fact, Holloway had sustained something close to a direct hit from an enemy bomb while travelling in his car late in 1940. He was rescued from the vehicle in serious condition and taken to hospital, but he was sufficiently recovered to lead the first team during the whole of the following year. Indeed, Holloway literally nursed the club though the war. Too old for active service, he kept things going, financially and in the sporting sense, through perhaps the most difficult years in its history.

Increasingly, membership was depleted and selection affected by the war. Players would be called away days or even hours before the scheduled start of a game. Others would appear just as suddenly, home on leave for a few hours and anxious to wield a bat or turn an arm. Austin, Bills, Booty and Chappell were among the senior players who came and went as members of the armed forces. One who was destined not to return was the very capable batsmen Pilot Officer Jack Lynn, who joined the RAF at the beginning of the conflict. In August came news that he had been lost following a successful bombing raid on Germany. He had joined the club in its most successful post First World War year, 1933, making just a few appearances for the 3rd eleven, with a best score of 79 against Forest Hill. After a few average seasons he became a leading run maker with the Seconds, with occasional sorties into the First XI, and in 1937 was elected to the Committee. In that year he was second to LW Black in the 2nd XI averages, with best scores of 69 against Chiswick Park and 62 against Spencer. In 1938 he joined Burrough, Cutter and Standerwick among 2nd XI century makers. In 1938 he averaged exactly 40 with a precise 100 against Maori (in a 181 partnership with JS Standerwick) and 89 against that most redoubtable of Cyphers' opponents, Beddington. There was no time for an entry into the statistics in 1939. He was one of the first members to join up and, as far as the record shows, the first to die in his country's service. A lesser known casualty was Flying Officer WH Humphreys, who briefly kept wicket for the club in 1938 and scored 108n.o. against KC&G, 50 against Stoics and 79 against Lloyds Bank in Cricket Week of that year, before moving to Gravesend for whom he played just as briefly and with as much promise.[1]

By this time, difficulties experienced in maintaining the front pitch caused the committee to abandon 'A' matches on the usual wicket. Instead, two sides shared the rather makeshift and less precious piece of ground at the rear of the clubhouse which was used generally by the 'B' side. With fuel for the motor mower unobtainable, horses were brought in to mow and roll the outfield and square. And competition for that excessively used turf increased with the announcement of a Cyphers Junior side under the captaincy of a young player who had quickly established himself in the 'A' team, JW (John) Duncan. Here, in the darkest days of war, was founded a side that would provide some of the club's best cricketers in the days of war and peace that lay ahead. For the present, schoolboys and young leavers who made up the Junior XI acquitted themselves well against others in much the

[1] *Evening Standard*, 11 June 1940, Flying Officer Humphreys reported missing believed killed

same position as themselves. Many had been compelled to depart their schools earlier than expected because of the evacuation, the disappearance of staff and pupils to remote places. By 1942, a Cyphers Cadet Corps was formed and a battery was operating alongside the balloon detachment on the front pitch.[2]

There was an octagonal quality to the 'A' fixtures, eight won, eight lost and eight drawn, a statistic that is leavened by three abandoned matches. Four players between them accounted for most of the runs – Jenner, Wisdom, Wardle and Duncan – without any of them reaching the century mark in a single match. WR Burrough, who was able to play only ten matches altogether, hit 54 in his second game and a newcomer, PB Smith, made 50 in his first match. Jenner had exceeded the 1000 runs mark in 1940 but in 1941, despite heading the averages at a shade over 29, was confined to an aggregate of 611. Deteriorating pitches with slow outfields were blamed in a committee report. It was noted that a well-known host side was worse off than Cyphers. There, it was said, out fielders found themselves in grass up to their knees!

õ

One remarkable feature of the war period was the continued ability of club cricket to attract the public. Even though the senior side played on the back pitch, and even though proceedings had to compete at times with aerial dog-fights and daytime bomb attacks – Biggin Hill was just along the road – a faithful band of citizens

---

[2] John Duncan to author, *ibid.* He added the melancholy footnote that of the 16 or 18 junior cricketers he had to choose from, 7 or 8 did not survive the war.

still turned out at Kings Hall Road, more especially when 'Whizz' was batting. His majestic sixes had become famous in club circles and beyond. One much respected local player, Leslie Pearce, whose church-founded team Christchurch provided competition for many junior elevens and was a nursery for some top class players, often recalled the wartime Saturdays (and weekends long after) when word would be passed along the nearby bank grounds, 'Whizz's batting', and players waiting to bat joined members of the public in trotting along the road to Cyphers for an almost guaranteed display of round-the-wicket hitting. Leslie Pearce's recollection was confirmed by many another local, though most are gone now to play their cricket on Elysian turf.

Things had changed drastically by 1941. Cricket – and a good quality of cricket at that – had survived. But there were no more Cricket Weeks, no more Bank Holiday or Whit Monday fixtures, no more free teas or subsidised beer at the Bank of England or the oil company grounds. Pavilion lights that had once illuminated after-match hospitality and occasional 'ladies nights' were now blacked out. It was all very tentative, low key and cognisant of larger concerns. Since early in 1940, the front pitch was taken over as a barrage balloon site and cricket had to be played on the back field. The pavilion had been commandeered by the RAF who operated the barrage balloon and slept in the main changing rooms, though the club was allowed to use about half the available space. Towards the end of 1940 an anti-aircraft shell penetrated the pavilion roof and hit the RAF sleeping quarters. Fortunately, all personnel were at their duty stations and no one was killed or injured.

Back to fact and figures. All-rounder Wardle was still prominent in the batting and bowling tables. This year he took 85 wickets, against 42 the season before; then they cost 17.43 runs each, now 8.24. He was joined by Cecil Tinsley and EA Griffin, bowling more than a hundred overs and taking 43 and 20 wickets respectively. NP Reeves's spasmodic appearances brought him 17 wickets at just over 10 runs apiece. Five old stagers kept the 'B' going – Robbins, AR Beardwell, Waddington, Eastwood, and Gerosa – assisted mainly by John Duncan's juniors. Their record was disappointing. 'The bald facts are', said the report... 'of 20 matches played, 2 were won, 4 drawn and 14 lost'. Only the veteran AR Beardwell scored over 200 runs. And his son HA, Howard (like 'Whizz' an old Alleynian), made what the Australians would call his debut, with 62 runs from five innings, at an average of 15.5, second to EB Thornton in the annual list; AR was third behind Howard. The Beardwell dynasty now stretched to four active members. Only one fifty was made — by KG White. There was better report of the bowling. Gerosa took 47 wickets at an itemised cost 8.17; TE Rockliff, JC Waddington, EG Eastwood, and NP Reeves all took more than 20 wickets.

Much better team and individual performances marked the 1942 season. The skipper of the 'A' Eleven, Rupert Holloway, made 388 runs in 13 appearances to finish a season shortened by injury at the top of the averages, with 43.1. A consistent batsman and outstanding fielder, Holloway had seldom been out of the first half dozen in the club averages since he took over the captaincy in 1930, but this was the first time on record that he achieved first place as a batsman. Wisdom was less than a single run behind him, with 639 from 19 innings. A newcomer, FW Parker, headed the bowling averages with figures of 154o 21m 566r 51w 11.1ave. A remarkable entry. He was followed by more familiar names, Allen, Gerosa, Wardle, Tinsley. But it was the depth of batting and bowling achievement that marked the year's senior team performance. Beckenham, the old enemy, were bowled out for 74 in reply to Cyphers' 173 for 9 in the opening match of the season. A new player, R Spice (48) and Rupert Holloway (51) were top scorers.

By the following year, 1943, the war had begun to take serious toll of the fixture list. The 'A' eleven played 32 games, mostly against scratch local sides, including Croydon and Catford Police and the RAOC. Twelve of those fixtures were won, eight lost, one tied and eleven drawn.

As captain of the Bs, AR Beardwell was able to give vent to some small satisfaction as well as to his own disciplinarian philosophy when he handed to the hon secretary a cryptic contribution to the annual report: 'A very successful season. Better batting, better bowling, but strange lapses in the fielding. Please stress this.' He left it to the Hon Sec. to add to the report that his son Howard, after playing in the first match of the season, scoring 17 runs and taking one catch, had gone off to the army, was commissioned and sent to France and, in August, was severely wounded. The same report thanked Howard's mother, Mrs AR Beardwell, for her services as scorer to both the first and second elevens. Post war players and their wives and girl friends would have more cause to remember Mrs Beardwell as the Lady of the Kitchen, ruling over the tea ceremonies and 'all-day' match feasts with a rod of iron. Nothing was allowed to come between the Beardwells and Cyphers. Flying Officer PA Chappell also appeared briefly for the club after an outstanding record at the County School in hockey, cricket and rugby, before joining the RAF and being reported missing in action. 'May he be safely returned', wrote AR Beardwell in his Captain's report. It was not to be. He was officially reported 'lost' in October 1943, and the local newspaper recorded that he was the first baby to be born at Beckenham's first maternity home in Croydon Road, 23 years before. He was also one of four brothers, another of whom had died in an air raid after escaping from Dunkirk.[3] BP Holloway, a nephew of the club Captain, had played on and off for the 2nd and 3rd elevens in 1937/8, before he too became an early volunteer for military service.

The glimmer of light that had shone fitfully in each year's wartime report, became an optimistic beam by the summer of 1944. 'The Cricket Section of the Cyphers Club entered on its fifth – and what most or all of its members believe to be the last – season of the European War with a full list of fixtures for two teams.' By winter, all had changed. 'Fate', said the report, '(and Hitler) ruled that barely half of the programme should be fulfilled; and ironically enough the summer of victory proved to be the worst summer for the Club.'

The indiscriminate 'doodle-bug' campaign was in full flood by mid June, and it had already become apparent that South-East London was a prime target. For groups of people to occupy public spaces was patently dangerous and foolhardy. All matches were cancelled from the middle of June. The position would be reviewed in August with the intention of resuming play in September if other clubs could be persuaded to do likewise.

Õ

---

[3] *Beckenham Journal* 16th October 1943.

By June, the irrepressible Whizz was in the thick of things in Palestine serving with the RAF at Ain Shomer, quaintly listed in RAF Daily Orders as 'Ein Shemer', for whom Wisdom is shown as having scored 47 out of a total of 115. The opposition, RAF Hadera, got the runs with two wickets down. RAF Ain Shomer soon became the centre of forces cricket in the country and Whizz found himself among several outstanding club and county players. Names like Chessman, McIntyre and Young showed up regularly in the CO's daily orders, alongside Wisdom. Sweet indeed was victory over the Haifa Police, a force fashioned by the redoubtable RGB Spicer who captained St Paul's School in his time and made cricket into a religion in the Palestine Police.

In May 1945 the *Beckenham Journal* reported: 'LAC EM Wisdom, well-known Cyphers cricketer, played his first game of the season for the R.A.F. in Palestine recently. Going in second he knocked up 68 before retiring'. Whizz was by now a star of the *Palestine Post's*[4] sports page.

In fact, conditions back home had not improved by the 1944 season's end and the ever-present danger was underlined when in January 1945 a V2 rocket hit the snow-clad cricket outfield where the balloon crew dugout had been until recently, close by the bowling green. It caused considerable damage to the bowls pavilion. The indoor bowls rink, then serving as a food store, was demolished and a number of people inside the building were

---

[4] *Palestine Post*, 17 May 1945. As might be expected, EM Wisdom topped his Station's averages with 56.20, most matches being played at a temperature of 96 degrees F plus. He was selected for the Northern area RAF side.

injured and taken to hospital.[5] Further home games, it seemed, would be impossible for some time to come.

Sudden victory came with the next summer, however, and for the first time in six years club cricket could be played once more without fear. Some members remained in the forces and only two teams could be raised, and that with difficulty. But the old fixtures returned – the likes of Gravesend, Richmond, Lloyds Bank, NatProv, all lost in wartime – and players came back from duty and injury to resume as best they could the game they had given up six years before. One who did not return was a young player of real promise, Fl/Lt Ken Banks. He was killed in a flying accident shortly after the end of hostilities had been declared. His last game with the club had been for the seconds in 1941. And there were other losses. EG (Gerry) Gerosa, the most clubbable of club cricketers, had died in February 1944 after enduring a terminal illness with something close to good humour. He was the kind of player who was unconcerned as to which side he played in, where he batted or fielded, whether or not he was asked to bowl, though he performed all such tasks with distinction in both 'A' and 'B' sides throughout the war. The Club's wartime President, Percy Hodes, whose son had been killed in action, also died early in the same year to the distress of those who knew him and his work through the 'thirties and the war years. Rupert Holloway, Captain and ambassador of the club for ten years, was elected to take his place.

The two sides still shared the back pitch while vital work on the front ground and pavilion was carried out. Yet, despite all the planning and logistical problems, every Saturday from the last

---

[5] *Beckenham Journal*, 13th January 1945.

week in April to the third in September was fully booked up. Specially organised games against Beckenham commemorated VE and VJ days. The first eleven played 33 matches, including Bank Holiday and special fixtures, winning 11, drawing 13 and losing 9. But the first summer of peace was a wet one and four matches had to be abandoned. A memorable match against Westminster Bank marked the return to near normal cricket. It was played on August Bank Holiday and the opposition batted first and scored 210 for 2 by the interval declaration. Cyphers had 20 minutes less batting time than the bank but set about the task with conviction. Tom Jenner, with a chanceless 51, set the pace. The decisive innings, however, was that of a young player who had appeared briefly for the Seconds in 1944, EG Purnell. He scored a superbly crafted 87. At the start of the last over the scores were level. The bat was surrounded by fielders. PB Smith, a regular through the war years, faced and hit the first ball to the boundary to secure victory.

New players and old hands came together in the prelude to Cyphers' most glorious years.

The batting, still led by Jenner, was strong and Purnell was about to add new force to it. Jimmy Black was still a solid opener. Norman Pedgrift, a good spin bowler and bat, and opening bowler Frank Dorset had lost none of their authority; and old hands like WA Wardle and Archie Perry, came well up in the batting figures, though the indomitable Wardle had begun to fade and would shortly become a powerful regular with the Third XI. His son Jim, who began playing for the club in the early part of the war, was to prove a worthy successor. Tinsley and Baignet also shone among the bowlers. In short, the First XI approached the summit of its considerable potential when war came and afterwards it had lost little of its strength. Only the Seconds' record spoilt the party in the first days of peace. Of 23 matches played they won not a single game. Howard Beardwell, home on leave from his army posting at Dover, enjoyed a few games with them and was the only member of the side to exceed 50 runs in a match. Against Beckenham in 1945, three Beardwells batted at six, seven and eight; Howard went for 50, his father AR for 1 and his uncle AE was not out 1.

õ

1946 was the year of transition: the year that saw the return of most of the members who had gone to war and survived; the year that saw the last of some eminent performers with willow and leather, and the advent of others. By the end of the season the selection committee that had so recently struggled to raise two sides could announce a strength of seventy playing members, of whom a mere dozen remained in the armed forces. A third XI was in being by the end of May, and soon a fourth XI was on occasional call. George Wager returned in time to prepare the front wicket for a full season's intensive wear, though he struggled with the back pitch. With rain and a broken motor mower to add to the woes of wartime blemish, it was generally reckoned that he performed miracles of repair in 1946.

Now combining Presidency with Captaincy, Rupert Holloway was, in fact, able to lead the side on only seven occasions. He was one of several players whose injuries sustained in war were to lead to the curtailment of some promising cricket careers. Most significant by far in that respect was TC Johnston's brief return to the club. As we have seen, in his last season before his war service, he continued to dominate both batting and bowling. Even now, handicapped by persistent injury, he averaged 20.75 from four appearances at the crease and topped the bowling figures for the season with twelve wickets from 47 overs at the remarkable cost of 6.91 each. Surely such an all-round talent would have much, much more to offer the game, even perhaps at first class level. But it was not to be. He registered his address in Cyphers' records as Romford, Essex. Whether he went back to old haunts, succumbed to injury or simply gave up the game that he had graced so spectacularly, the record fails to show. In any event, he was never heard of again in Cyphers' annals.

He was in good company. This was the year in which two of the greatest of all cricketers bade farewell, Bradman and Hammond. For cricketers everywhere, whatever their standard of play, there was some comfort in the plight of the great men, of Bradman's dismissal on his last visit to the crease in England at the hand of Hollies, when tears surely clowded his eyes; of Hammond's decline when fibrositis set in after a test career comprising 6,000 runs in 129 innings, 22 centuries, 100 catches, and 80 wickets. Even the gods must succumb eventually.

Following Holloway's temporary exclusion, Tom Jenner led the side to impressive double victories over Sutton and Westminster Bank. Old names and familiar performances began to fill the score books – Jenner (715 runs, 108 against Sutton, and an average of 37.63), LW Black (550, ave. 34.37), Wisdom (477, ave. 25.1), Bills (314, ave. 28.54) – but it was the promise contained in less familiar entries that called for special notice: Perry (449, ave.24.94), Purnell (497, 106n.o. against Streatham, ave.23.66), and not least by any means, FJ Kelsh, a brilliant all-rounder who had spent much of the war as a rear-gunner in the RAF, and came up the line from Catford as it were. In his first year the off-spinner Kelsh was second in the bowling figures to the irrepressible Johnston, with 58 wickets from 199 overs (ave. 10.65). Another of the newcomers, JAF Crawford, was in third place above such experienced players as Wardle Snr, Tinsley and Parker, with an average of 12.42 from 69 overs. It all augured well. Peace seemed finally to have blossomed. Cyphers must unveil a salutary plaque on the pavilion wall and, like most other institutions in the United Kingdom, pull itself up by the boot straps.

õ

IN PROUD AND HONOURED MEMORY OF THE
MEMBERS OF THIS CLUB WHO LOST THEIR LIVES
THROUGH ENEMY ACTION
1914 – 1918   1939 – 1945

J ALEXANDER - GH BAKER - KJ BANKS - PA CHAPPELL
- F HALL - WF HAZELGROVE - PH HODES (JNR) - JC LYNN -
GK RADCLIFFE - NP REEVES - CA RODGERS - LL ROWE - F
SNAZELL - HC STEMBRIDGE - F THORPE - GA WARDLE -
CH YOUNG

4

Post War

In cricket as in most things war wrought great changes. Its aftermath carried in train a new approach to those sporting and leisure activities that were once the preserve of the well off and privileged.

As the club prepared for its first full year of peace, there was a momentary look over the shoulder when Rupert Holloway announced a scheme to place bench seats round the front pitch, each dedicated to a member who had given his life in the conflict. They had forgotten Flying Officer Humphreys on the memorial plaque but remembered him with a commemorative seat.

One of the most apposite developments of the immediate post-war period at King's Hall Road was the formation of the Cyphers Choir, which soon achieved something of a reputation locally. Its founder and inspiration was Ernest Hall, a prominent bowls player and, more to the point, first trumpet in the BBC Symphony Orchestra and Professor of that instrument at the RCM.

A Grand Supper Dance at the Eden Park Hotel in February 1947, offered newcomers the chance to meet old hands and each other. Some familiar names were still there – Jenner, Black, Bills, Wisdom, the Beardwells, Wardle, Newton, Parker, and so on – but gradually the batting line ups began to take different shape; and new trundlers, spinners and would-be speed men appeared, but the cry still went out for a really effective strike bowler. It would not be long before the club enjoyed something of an embarrassment of such riches. Those who once would have played soccer but hardly ever cricket came into the game. Over the years recruits from a disintegrating empire would appear, and some of them who had learnt their skills on matting and grassless wickets would assuredly fill any remaining spin and fast bowling gaps. But such thoughts anticipate an ambivalent future. At the start of the 1947 season, four elevens took the field from the first Saturday, and Sunday fixtures became a regular feature for the first time in the club's history.

The traditional opener against Beckenham ended in a win for Cyphers in the First XI game, but victory wasn't to be the herald of great things. A hard fought draw against Banstead, in which only the newcomer Kelsh reached double figures, was followed by one drawn game after another and defeats at the hands of Dulwich, Spencer (by ten wickets) and Addiscombe. Only rare victory and the occasional shambles lifted the gloom. The Dulwich match was shown in the fixture list as a home game for the First XI and away for the Seconds. The mistake was corrected on the selection sheet posted in the pavilion, but no one thought to tell the scorer. Grant duly arrived at King's Hall Road to be greeted by 2nd XI skipper Dave Bonner. Told of the mix up, Grant rushed to the nearest bus stop and proceeded towards Dulwich.

Cyphers were almost all in the pavilion by the time he arrived at the Turney Road ground. They were all out for 95 and Dulwich made the runs with five wickets to spare. Grant versified:

> The Cyphers lost last Saturday,
> And they are asking - WHY?
> Was it because their Fixture List
> Contained a little lie?
>
> In days gone by when things went wrong
> The team was in a plight,
> The scorer offered up a prayer
> That sometimes put things right.
>
> No prayers he offered up that day
> For he was feeling sore.
> Their Fixture List led him astray
> They were past praying for!
>
> The moral is, in future games
> At Home or else Away,
> You'd better let the Scorer know
> Where you intend to play.

A washed out opening game against the Wanderers, defeats at the hands of Gravesend and strong MCC and London University sides, and draws with Beckenham, Spencer and Streatham, made up the Cricket Week picture in July. New names jostled with old.

Batting

	ings	n.o.	runs	highest score	ave
EM Wisdom	35	4	1090	102*	35.16
TH Jenner	27	2	851	100*	34.04
HA Beardwell	18	3	498	100*	33.20
A Perry	22	4	534	84*	29.66
MDJ McGrath	16	5	308	68	28.00
GS Tyers	13	1	330	85*	27.50
LW Black	21	-	572	100	27.23
FW Kettle	29	4	675	99	27.00
DB Evans	17	4	346	73*	26.61
JW Duncan	24	3	533	68	25.38
GW Higgs	9	1	183	57	22.87
FJ Kelsh	27	3	538	97	22.41

Bowling

	overs	maidens	runs	wcks	ave
J Eastwood	37.3	8	114	11	10.36
NF Pedgrift	53.4	16	175	16	10.93
LW Latter	186.2	22	602	52	11.57
CE Cutter	120	12	407	34	11.97
JD Griffin	63	20	160	13	12.31
AE Beardwell	63.1	9	217	17	12.76
P Duncan	108.4	13	411	31	13.25
GV Firmin	48	9	146	11	13.27
EM Wisdom	34	3	120	9	13.33
JA Bills	84	16	230	17	13.58
JW Duncan	59	3	231	17	13.58

The Firsts won six and lost nine of the 28 games played. The rest were drawn. The Second and Fourth elevens both won more games than they lost. Some hope for the future resided in that. Overall, in fact, the club won 46, lost 43 and drew 37 in its first real year of peacetime endeavour. Rupert Holloway in his captain's report bemoaned as ever the lack of a good fast bowler and the weight of responsibility that rested on the broad shoulders of Wardle and Kelsh. But he saw promise in the intermittent appearances of Parker and Crawford. The single appearance of WA Dorset when on leave from the RAF, augured well, he thought. 'He will be a great asset on his return to civilian life'. The 2nd XI came out on top, winning eleven matches against six lost. The 3rd XI won nine and lost thirteen. The combined 4th and occasional 5th elevens won twelve and lost nine.

A better scenario was in store for 1948. Old guard and new boys combined at the start of the season to inflict decisive defeats on Beckenham, Banstead, Sutton, and Kenley, traditionally among the club's strongest opponents. Jenner, Coles, Wardle, Wisdom and Black, were all among the runs early on. But it was Kelsh the all-rounder who did the most spectacular damage, often abetted by Parker. Kelsh's 4 for 52 against Beckenham, 4 for 12 against Banstead, 5 for 32 against Kenley, 5 for 41 against Lloyds Bank, were figures that would stand out in any company. Wardle was not to be overshadowed: 4-88 at Foxgrove Road, 5-11 against Westminster Bank at home, 5-54 at Sutton, 5-72 against Lloyds Bank. By mid June, however, the brakes had been applied. The return game with Banstead was lost, Streatham had an easy win and Beddington had the best of a close finish. Victories over Stoics and London University raised spirits in Cricket week but headlines like 'Cyphers tired fielding' did nothing to sustain confidence. There was another famous victory, this time over Old Whitgiftians in that club's Cricket Week. OW's number four bat, still at the school though playing for the old boys in the holidays, would become a familiar name in the near future, R Subba Row. On this occasion he distinguished himself more as a bowler, with 5 for 69.

A piece by Tom Barling in the *Evening Standard* a few months later makes interesting retrospective reading:

> R SUBBA ROW, aged 17, of Whitgift Grammar School. This boy, an Indian, bats left hand and shows great promise. He plays well in front of the wicket, especially on the off-side. Because he moves his feet so well he takes full toll of anything short, getting right behind the ball before making his shot. Actually, he does not get the amount of runs he should, for undoubtedly he has the ability. I do not think he concentrates enough, which may account for lapses which cost him his wicket more than once last season when he seemed well set.[1]

At the end of the season, Cyphers Firsts had won 10 and lost 5 of their matches, and drawn 10, thus reversing the previous year's trend. First and foremost, as the annual report said, vice-captain FJ Kelsh created a club record: 110 wickets in the season, four more than WA Wardle's previous record established in 1943. The Third XI had set the pace, however, with 16 wins and only 2 losses and 2 draws. The Fourth XI had done almost as well, 12 wins, 6 losses and 3 draws.

An omen for all who believe that eccentricity is a vital ingredient of the club game was the advent towards the end of the

---

[1] *Evening Standard*, 9 May 1949.

1948 season of a regular Fifth XI, a repository for all the skills of bygone years, though perhaps past their prime, and all the optimism of raw youth.

The indefatigable Jenner still topped the batting averages but he was followed by several new names, notable SJ Coles and EG Purnell. Wisdom occupied an alien 28th place. Someone, somewhere would surely pay for his unaccustomed rating.

Rupert Holloway's own performances had slumped in the post war years and he had never been fully fit since his wartime accident. At the approach of the 1949 season he decided to relinquish the captaincy. He was immediately elected to the chairmanship of the club he had served so well and for so long. In the vote to replace him as skipper of the Firsts there was near unanimous support for Wisdom, the man who – along with only three other players, Jenner, WA Wardle and AR Beardwell – had exceeded 10,000 runs for the club and was destined to score more than anyone and whose example on and off the field was widely admired. It proved a profitable choice.

The year of Whizz's initiation as captain marked Cyphers' sixtieth anniversary and its most successful season.

'Remarkable bowling by Kelsh. Cyphers dismiss Beckenham for 45'. The *Beckenham Journal*[2] greeted the first of the 1949 season's matches with bold type and bold prose. Then: 'Cyphers fielding was good. Banstead all out for 58', and 'Sutton fall victims to Cyphers bowlers'. So the story went on. The matches were mostly low scoring on both sides. There were some notable batting displays: 131 by GW Higgs against Beddington Seconds, 125 not out by Jenner against Dulwich, 123 from Purnell in the

---

[2] *Beckenham Journal* 30 April 1949 *et al.*

MCC Cricket Week match, and 123 from FW Kettle against Wanstead Seconds, 117 from Black against Kenley, centuries on two consecutive days by JW Duncan in July. But the bowling was scaling new heights. Kelsh and newcomer Dorset made a mighty contribution to a succession of victories. Kelsh 8 for 6, Dorset 2 for 33, were the Beckenham analyses. Dorset 4 for 24, Kelsh 5 for 34, against Kenley. Kelsh 7 for 48, Dorset 3 for 65, against Westminster Bank. In some matches that pair were bowled by the new skipper unchanged through the opposition innings. On other occasions they were joined by Parker and JAF Crawford, exceptionally by Purnell and another newcomer, all-rounder Higgs. There was a decisive victory over Stoics in Cricket Week, and a two run win against a strong MCC side containing Blake, Tyrwitt-Drake, Devereux, Rex Alston and Freddie Titmus.

The first two months of the year saw remarkable individual and team performances. Wisdom's influence certainly showed in the first part of 1949. His own batting seemed to be suffering, however, perhaps from war service, perhaps from age or over exposure; at any rate he began to send himself in at number seven, and as with everything else in the new order of things, the ends seemed for the moment to justify the means. By the week end of July 11, the local press was erroneously reporting the loss of a Cricket Week game against Catford. Incensed readers, proud of the club's hundred per cent record, protested that the match was drawn and an apology appeared the next week.[3] It was not until September 10th, almost at the end of the season, that Cyphers' astonishing record was spoiled. 'One-handed catch gave Gravesend Victory', said a *Journal* headline, 'Cyphers have lost

---

[3] *Beckenham Journal*, 16 July 1949

their record'. 'Gravesend's three run victory with the last ball of the match'[4] was a thrilling end, all the same, to a splendid year's cricket. Well, almost. There was one other defeat before the season ended. Old Whitgiftians, benefiting from a dropped catch off their number eleven, were able to achieve a single wicket victory. Wins over Dulwich, Richmond and Beddington brought the season to the best overall resolution in the club's history. Jenner, who hit 125 not out against Dulwich, as was his wont these days, took first place in the 1st XI batting averages. After a faltering start, Ted Purnell's season proved the best since he joined the club in the last year of war, and he registered the highest aggregate of runs, 959. A truly imperious manner at the wicket and a commanding presence in the field caused all the old hands, particularly Rupert Holloway, to look on 'Pym' Purnell as a bat who would grace club and representative cricket for a long time to come. In fact, Holloway recommended the very promising young player to Lords and at the start of the next season Ted began his eight games induction for *The Club*.

But no one paid much attention to batting achievements at this stage. It was bowling that caught the eye:

	overs	maidens	runs	wickets	average
FJ Kelsh	516.2	153	131	1153	8.80
JA Crawford	215.5	34	46	664	14.43
FW Parker	87.2	10	19	284	14.94
WA Dorset	340.5	63	60	1009	16.81

---

[4] ibid, Aug-Oct 1949

In that evolutionary process which sees the great ones of the past handing on their enthusiasm and skill to new generations, AR Beardwell, who had played for the club since 1920, took over the captaincy of the now firmly established 5th XI. This was the side in which old masters were put out to grass and youngsters cut their teeth. Playing under Beardwell Snr was as tough and exacting as it would have been playing for the 1st or 2nd XI, and discipline was just as severe. Many would had cause to thank him as they progressed in the game, and not a few would rue their indiscretions.

The winning streak continued well into 1950. The local newspaper headlines again found in cricket the kind of copy that normally went with the winter's football antics -- 'Fine Cyphers win over Banstead', 'Cyphers in Great Form', '100 Up in 58 Minutes, Cyphers Openers in Great Form'; 'Dorset bowls well for Cyphers – Gallant Beddington attempt fails'; the *presto* mood became *diminuendo* when a draw was all that could be offered the back page reader, 'Hopes of win dispelled – Cyphers draw with Kenley'.[5] But soon the scent of local ascendancy was in the air again. In mid July the *Evening Standard* reported another 'brilliant win', this time over Beckenham in the last game of Cricket Week. There had already been decisive wins over London University, Stoics, Wanderers and WA Davidson's XI. In the Stoics match, a low scoring encounter, Subba Row made the most runs on either side with 39 for the opposition; Wisdom, caught Cape bowled Subba Row, was one run behind him. As for the Beckenham match:

---

[5] *Beckenham Journal*, May 20 - July 15 1950.

> Cyphers forced a brilliant victory over their visitors, Beckenham...
> Set to make 167 in a 100 minutes after tea they won by three
> wickets with a few moments to spare...Cyphers left no doubt that
> they meant to go for the runs. EG Purnell, in a slightly rearranged
> batting order, opened with Black. PSM Auld bowled to Purnell
> who took 12 off the first over, and 50 came in 29 minutes...[6]

This was the period of the *Evening Standard* Club Cricket Competition, in which North and South London tables of leading clubs' results gave rise to an end of season final. By the end of July, Alexandra Park and Cyphers led their respective sections, though only Ilford at that stage could equal Cyphers' record of not a single game lost.[7]

As with most good things, the end was not only inevitable, it was bloody. Spencer started the rot in August with a three-wicket victory at Wandsworth. There were narrow wins for Cyphers against Streatham, Westminster Bank and Sutton, and a draw with Midland Bank, before Nat Prov and Old Whitgiftians delivered the final *coup.* The former won narrowly, by 15 runs, the latter massively, R S-Row in his bowling role taking 9 for 24 in Cyphers' total of 43 all out. A four-wicket win by Beddington in the traditional last game brought down the curtain on a season that had promised much but which fizzled out in rain and some desperately untypical batting; batting that saw Wisdom going in at number nine and an unfit Kelsh, who only a season before had opened with Jenner, occupying the number eleven position. Second and First eleven players, FJ Ridout and JW Duncan, headed the club averages with 38.05 and 31.21 respectively.

---

[6] *Evening Standard*, 17 July 1950

[7] ibid, 25 July 1950

Bowling as in the season before was the highlight of all the sides' performances, with another Dorset, Frank, taking 9 for 35 against Lloyds Bank IV, another 4th XI player AM Postgate 8 for 35 against Cuaco III; WA Wardle, now with the Seconds, had some astonishing figures, as the captain's report said 'despite his age', including 8 for 15 against Cuaco, 6 for 14 against Kenley, and 6 for 59 against Spencer. Kelsh, although reaching only half way in the club bowling table for the year, had early season figures of 7 for 47 against Stoics, 6 for 49 against Dulwich. It was an indifferent season but it was the harbinger of another of Wisdom's golden years of captaincy - Festival of Britain year.

It was the year when England ended Australia's unbroken run of post-war test victories, when Hutton and Co, under the amateur captaincy of Freddie Brown, at last brought home the loot of war. Reg Simpson, David Sheppard, Trevor Bailey and John Dewes were other members of the side who were designated 'amateur' on the day's scorecards. Whizz had a special regard for Hutton's batting and kept press cuttings of most of his test match achievements. He seems to have found tactical inspiration in the 1951 series in Australia.

Perhaps it was that. Perhaps it was the euphoria of Festival Year, the year in which Britain set out to demonstrate to the world that it could breath and flex its muscles again after the tribulations of war. Perhaps it was the coming together of a side that had been an uneasy amalgam of past and present since 1946. Perhaps it was the appearance of a new bowling phenomena in a side that was already overflowing with bowling talent. Whatever the reason, it may as well be said at the outset, as the Committee report would say at the end, the First Eleven flag 'was not lowered in any Saturday match'.

Much credit must assuredly be given to the young school teacher with a mop of dark hair, well-tuned northern accent and magical fingers who turned up at the start of the season. His name was John Iberson. He had won a place at University College, Oxford, in his last school year but had joined the RAF as a bomber pilot before going to Univ. He was on his way to teach at St Dunstan's School, with something of a reputation as a left-arm wrist and finger spinner of googlies and off breaks, or 'chinas' in the language of the trade.

'LUSTY BATTING BY CYPHERS – Black hits a century – then Iberson takes 5 for 9.' Thus did the *Beckenham Journal's* back page summarise the opening game with Beckenham. The Dulwich fixture was an honourable draw, though 'Iberson's bowling success' was the headline. A somewhat disappointing 4 for 45. Then came Cricket Week in July, with defeat at the hands of London University, with heavy guns such as Dujon making the necessary runs with only three wickets down, a high scoring draw against Stoics, a large defeat by the Wanderers who scored 263 for 7 decl. and bowled out Cyphers for 173, and a rain spoilt match against an MCC side containing Peter May and actor-cricketer Trevor Howard. The scorecard is worthy of preservation:

Cyphers

FJ Kelsh c Laws b Davidson	92
LW Black b May	56
NF Pedgrift c Laws b Davidson	24
EG Purnell c Buckland b Roberts	36
FE Brigden c May b Davidson	62
EM Wisdom not out	20
Extras...	11
Total (for 5 wkts dec.)	301

MCC

Desmond Roberts c Black b Kelsh	12
LA Dunthorne c & b Kelsh	1
PBH May not out	56
ACE Smith b Dorset	2
HL Laws not out	7
Total (for 3 wickets)	<u>78</u>

JR Tovey, Maj JSW Meikle, Trevor Howard, HM Buckland, WA Davidson and HS Mather did not bat. Bowling Kelsh 2 for 36, Dorset 1 for 42.

That match was played on Saturday 14th July 1951. It was opposition of the kind that tests the strength of any club side and Kelsh's performance with bat and ball was enough to underline his all-round abilities in whatever company. A fortnight later, on Saturday 28th July, Peter May made his test match debut, scoring 110 not out in the Fourth Test against South Africa at Headingley. It is tempting to wonder what might have happened had the future England captain been able to continue his innings at King's Hall Road.

An even more interesting encounter followed on the last day of the Week. Cyphers were 9 wickets down before lunch for 92, the renowned Beckenham pair Wong and Schubert doing the damage, and were forced to declare because Iberson their number eleven was late, a not uncommon experience with 'Ibers', as cricket captains up and down the land were to discover. After lunch Beckenham were dismissed for 80 by the combined assault of Crawford and Dorset, 7 for 43 and 3 for 36 respectively. By mid afternoon the match was deemed to be over, but the umpires thought otherwise. Cricket is, after all, essentially a two innings affair, and the captains agreed to a second innings. Cyphers declared at 162 for 5. Beckenham were all out for 73, Kelsh taking 3 for 31 and Iberson, bearing lightly the responsibility for a complete change in the nature of the match, 7 for 40.

Iberson's dependence on public transport and his habit of turning up late – sometimes hours late – at the most important games with a paper bag containing his whites and boots, soon gave cause for alarm at Cyphers and among skippers of representative sides. Why couldn't he buy himself a car? After all, he wasn't badly paid as a master at a prominent public school. In fact, incongruity as much as eccentricity was part of John's charm as man and cricketer, and cricket would simply have to live with his determined individualism for some years to come. There was a widespread sigh of relief, none the less, when he met Alice, an Irish chemist, who became his wife when he was 39 and who introduced at least a measure of organisation to his life. In the meantime, it was Ted Purnell's wife Christine who was given the job of chauffeuse, collecting him usually from St Dunstan's, and ensuring his appearance in time to take the field lest the captain lost the toss. Remarkably for a wartime pilot, John had never learnt to drive a car, 'there's more room in the sky' he would say when challenged with his indifference to comfort and punctuality. Those who drove him soon learnt that his almost total preoccupation was with high finance. The movements of the stock market were of much more concern to him than bowling statistics (which he distrusted and despised). He wasn't mean, but he was respectful of money and knew the exact price of most things.

By late August, the club was once again the only unbeaten side in the *Evening Standard* league table. But it was second to South

Hampstead who had won more matches. This new, competitive feature was not altogether popular in club circles. Some saw it as the beginning of a process that would make winning an end in itself and deprive the club game of its true spirit. None the less, the table gave an interesting account of the state of the game north and south of the Thames six years after the end of hostilities. In the top six with Cyphers and S.Hampstead were Malden Wanderers, Old Whitgiftians, Beddington and Ealing. The bottom six was made up of Richmond, BBC, Brondesbury, Highgate, Hounslow and Old Citizens. Catford, Hornsey, Ilford and the Vine floated somewhere in the middle. With a last over win against Dulwich in September and a dramatic draw with Beddington, Cyphers retained their unique unbeaten record to the end but could only make third place; S.Hampstead remained top of the table and Old Whitgiftians gained second place with a string of late victories.

First team results would undoubtedly have been even better than is suggested by 10 wins, 3 losses (all in Cricket week and not included in *Evening Standard* figures), and 19 draws, had not Kelsh and Iberson both been called away to play for Kent II and Herts respectively at critical times. For the statistically minded, the annual Committee report's comparative averages, that is club figures against opponents', painted a bright picture; the 1st, 3rd and 4th elevens all ahead of the opposition, and only the 2nd and 5th elevens trailing. Such figures were substantiated by batting and bowling performances that at times were breathtaking, Black's 169 not out against Westminster Bank, and partnerships between Black and Jenner of 209 for the first wicket against the bank, and Black and HA Beardwell of 192 for the third wicket against Old Ardinians; the already mentioned bowling performances of Dorset, Crawford and Iberson[8]. And a batting display by the latest member of the Duncan family to play for the club, RA, should not be overlooked, 103 not out against Westminster Bank 4th XI. His score included 32 runs made in one over, a club record. Duncan's feat was complemented by EA Griffin's 8 for 21 bowling performance against Sidcup IV. In fact, Griffin came sixth overall in the bowling averages, just ahead of Iberson. At the head of the annual table was a host of lower eleven players, in order of precedence AR Purnell, John Duncan's younger brother Peter, 'Teddy' Cutter, John Eastwood, RRC Gumbrill — with figures ranging from 8.61 to 11.50. It wasn't by any means a representative season in terms of individual performances, but all augured well for Cyphers at the close of Festival Year.

Again, newspaper headlines conveyed something of the ups and downs of 1952. 'Kenley give Cyphers third defeat – Kelsh bowls 7 for 67 unchanged', 'Kelsh gets among the wickets again. Cyphers return to form – Banstead out for 75', 'Cyphers in Great Form Dismiss Dulwich – Kelsh and Iberson Bowl 11 Consecutive Maidens', 'Pedgrift Hits Century in Cyphers Week – and takes 4 for 17, Cyphers Visitors Stave Off Defeat – Gravesend Last Men Defy Bowling'.[9]

The Kenley defeat, the first to be inflicted by that club in living memory, stung Cyphers and its supporters, not least scorer Grant.

---

[8] Tony Stevens tells me he 'thinks' Iberson took 9 for 9 against Streatham at this time. I can find nothing in Committee or press reports to substantiate the claim, but I mention it in case I have overlooked something. *Author*

[9] *Beckenham Journal* 14 June - 26 July.

KENLEY

At Kenley by the Surrey hills,
It was a peaceful scene
With all the country far and wide
Was wrapped in Summer green.

A change came o'er that peaceful scene,
The Cyphers stock went down,
The colour bar had been imposed,
And Black was caught by Brown.

Then Graves appeared upon the scene
With news from Headingley,
I'll be the 'true man' of this side
He cried exultantly.

The score book tells of his success,
How he the wickets spread,
The blow that it does not record
Is seen on Norman's head.

And Kenley proud of their success
Drank many, many beers.
For they had won a match at last,
It took them thirty years.

Even the *Tatler* had heard of the deeds of Cyphers by now and included a picture of Whizz's merry men along with a note that carried some useful historical tit-bits[10].

---

[10] *Tatler and Bystander*, June 11, 1952

... Outstanding players in the between wars period who have worn the claret, silver and black blazer include A.W.R. Matthews, W.L.T. Webb, P.B. Wise, L.M. Simmons, captain for twenty years, the brothers A.R. and W.A. Beardwell, R. Holloway, a former captain and now President, E.A. Griffin, T.H. Jenner, N.P. Andrews and W.A. Wardle... The latter retired from regular cricket in 1950, at the age of sixty-seven, and during his long career was one of the best all-rounders in club cricket. Since the war, E.M. Wisdom has captained the club with prominent players in F.J. Kelsh and J. Iberson, who have both appeared for Kent in Minor Counties matches... One of the most successful years since the war was the 1949 season, when F.J.Kelsh captured 148 wickets and the club were only defeated twice in a programme of thirty-three matches. Five teams are fielded each Saturday...

In a season of vicissitude, however, it was the Beckenham local derby, played on Saturday July 12th in Cricket Week, that caused the greatest stir. So much so that scorer Grant collapsed with over excitement and had to be replaced in the scorers' box. With Dorset, Kelsh, Iberson, and Higgs, four of the most successful bowlers in club and minor counties cricket, turning out, Cyphers were expected to continue an unbroken run of post-war victories over their old rivals. As it was, OJ Wait of Beckenham stole the bowling honours. He bowled unchanged at one end throughout the Cyphers innings, ending up with 25 overs, 8 maidens, 40 runs, 7 wickets. The *Beckenham Journal*[11] headline ran: 'Beckenham Beat the Cyphers For First Time Since War'. But the *Evening Standard* best conveys the drama of the occasion.

---

[11] 19 July 1952.

...a finish so exciting that 68-year old Ernest Grant, scorer for opponents Cyphers, collapsed and had to be replaced. Mr Grant recovered later. He has missed only three games in 27 years' scoring for the Cyphers, and will be on duty next week-end. Scores he could not complete: Beckenham 102; Cyphers 85. [12]

All the tension was caused by Wait bowling two wicket maidens to dismiss Jenner and Wisdom and thus make Cyphers 29 for six at tea. Higgs and Brigden raised hopes after tea with a partnership of 40 odd. Then it was Higgs lbw b Wait 10, Brigden c Schubert b Wait 37 (collapse of Grant), Kelsh c Emus b Wait 0, Dorset b Wait 8, Iberson not out 2.

Things improved in August. Tail end drama continued, all the same, to invest Cyphers cricket with a public reputation it had seldom known. 'Cyphers Visitors Stave Off Defeat', the headline[13] for the 19th July game, encapsulated a finish in which Gravesend's last remaining pair, the brothers M and G O Gunn, with a quarter of an hour on the clock and 66 runs needed, held out against the combined attack of Kelsh, Dorset and Pedgrift. Then came victories over Spencer, Sutton, Midland Bank and NatProv. And on 1st August, the Bank Holiday fixture with Westminster Bank. The bank needed two to win with four wickets in hand when Dorset bowled the last over. The first ball bowled number 6 King; the second and third balls resulted in the run out of both 8 and 9, Steer and Dodsworth. Off the last ball, number 11 Lane backed up well and got home for an almost impossible and quite unnecessary single just before the wicket was broken and the match ended in a bizarre draw.

---

[12] *Evening Standard*, Tuesday July 15th, 1952.

[13] *Beckenham Journal*, 26 July 1952

Into September the same cliff-edge cricket prevailed. 'CYPHERS IN EXCITING ONE-RUN VICTORY – Kelsh hits stumps seven times'; then 'GRAVESEND HAD TO SAVE THE GAME', the opposition holding out at 130 for 9 in reply to Cyphers' 211 for three; the following week, Whitgifts 183 for 5 decl. Cyphers 137 for 8, Iberson uncommonly returning a figure of one for 60; and at the end of the month 'Cyphers Make Lowest Score', 67 all out in reply to Dulwich's 118.[14] Cyphers' performances in 1952 seemed to reflect chiefly on the side's batting line up. That most enduring of openers Jenner was beginning to show signs of age and wear. Often missing out altogether, frequently betraying that tell-tale sign of weariness, the close run out. More significantly still, 'Whizzy' was putting himself in to bat ever further down the order and making ever fewer runs. There was the occasional glimmer of the electrifying batsman of old, but in the whole of August and September he had scored only 31 runs and he decided to resign the club captaincy at the end of the season. It was the disappointing finale to a First XI career that had stretched across twenty-two years and produced some of the finest and most aggressive batting ever witnessed on club grounds.

A vacillating season was necessarily reflected in the club's position in the *Evening Standard* table[15]. The competition was now divided into North and South regions, with a final between the two section winners, and Cyphers was in an unfamiliar seventh place in the South. Beddington was top of the table and

---

[14] *Beckenham Journal*, 6-27 Sept 1952

[15] *Evening Standard*, 3 Sept 1952

beat Wanstead, virtually the Essex nursery in those days, in the final.

The annual report of the Cricket Committee pronounced another successful year under the captaincy of EM Wisdom, winning 11 matches, losing 7 and drawing 13. Its conclusions were not entirely borne out by the figures. 'The batting was again strong with TH Jenner in good form, ably supported by Purnell, Pedgrift, Black, and a new member, BHM Thompson, whose best effort was 109 not out in a total of 171 for 8 against Stoics, having opened the innings.' In fact, the honours in the overall club batting averages went to the Duncan family, 'brothers Bob and John being first and second with averages of 37.80 and 35.13 respectively'. In a year in which AR Purnell headed the club's overall bowling figures (for the second time and chiefly for the 4th XI) and Iberson was a mere fourth in the table, another Duncan, Peter, was ninth overall in that department

November 14 was the occasion of Stoic's annual dinner, and a special one for it marked the 75th birthday of a club that had been represented by some of the great players of the game, including AE Stoddart of Hampstead and England, CJ Kortright of Essex and RWV Robins. The two Cyphers players who had already joined such company, Austin and Wisdom, had held their places comfortably among the good, the great and the promising of their day. Others would follow suit. Though no record persists, we can be fairly certain that Stoics' anniversary dinner promised its usual conviviality and wet fare. Those Cyphers members who received the annual invitation to Westminster Bank's dinner at the Windsor Castle just by Victoria Station in the same month, with WA Dry Esq in the chair, might have had cause to consider the portent.

With Andy Sandham proposing the club's health, most will have risked it.

The cricket section accepted the challenge of the Cyphers' bowls section to a Sunday match on their turf. The bowlers won by 108 shots to 30, but outstanding performances by crickters Jim Black and Howard Beardwell received commendations.

At the annual meeting of the cricket section in November, Whizz formally resigned the captaincy, along with the skipper of the Second XI FW Parker. They were succeeded respectively by LW Black and WE 'Waddy' Wadman. Other club officials at this transitional time were Third XI captain CE Cutter, Fourth XI WH Carter, Fifth XI JN Eastwood; hon secretary RJS Booty, hon assistant secretary JW Duncan. The Winter of 1952 held other reminders of the passage of time. Two days before the meeting, on 25th November, Ernest Grant the First XI scorer died at his home in Penge. The *Evening Standard* had clearly been misinformed about his age. He was 74. Of course, Rupert Holloway and Whizz straight away wrote to his widow, but it was the son, Walter Grant, who replied, and in his letter[16] to Whizz he reminisced in a poignant way about matches he and his father had watched at King's Hall Road, and on opponents' grounds, in days gone by:

> Dear Mr Wisdom - We [mother and I] very much appreciated your letter and it is pleasant for us to know how my father was appreciated by the club. We know the other side of the picture - how much the club meant to him. He and I first supported the Cyphers from the grass bank on the roadside about 1924. Wardle and Holloway opened the batting and the Cyphers first XI

---

[16] 14 Dec 1952, from 125 Oakfield Road, Penge, SE20

[batting] continued with WR Beardwell, Webb, Bowater, Wise, Downing, Minter, Matthews, Swynford, Simmons... Shortly afterwards we graduated to the pavilion side and my father became an honorary member... On an August Bank Holiday over at the Westminster Bank ground my father thought I ought to learn how to score and I had a score-book in my hand for the first time. The Cyphers had no scorer at the time. Mr Simmons spotted me and asked me to score. Terrified I fled for parental protection! My father scored and very soon became the regular scorer. School activities soon diverted my attention but his loyalty never waned. The last game he missed, I believe, was in 1939 when I took my degree and even then he managed to see the closing overs... During the war and in these latter years... his pleasure and interest in the club if possible increased; it became a more permanent interest than any other. If you have appreciated his loyalty, he deeply appreciated the kindness and understanding he received from you and many others, particularly as he became more frail. It is good that he went through this last season with his usual unfailing regularity, and he entered upon the Winter months rather depressed as he felt it was really becoming too much and he would be unable to continue. We are glad that he never had to make the decision to give up scoring... We are sure, however, that it is the happiness which he shared with you and the club which he would most want remembered now, and of which his verses were a constant reminder. Thank goodness that when the club gave him a Dunhill pipe in 1938 the tragedy he envisaged happening to the scorer never occurred.

> When Whizzy in aggressive mood,
> He sixes seeks to swipe
> Oh spare the corner where he sits
> Lest you should hit his pipe.

Overall club performance in 1952 was little better than passable, 140 matches played by all sides, 51 won, 48 lost, 41 drawn; though the Firsts were well above low water mark with 31 victories and 11 losses from 31 games. In fact, the 3rd XI did best with 11 wins and only 4 losses from 20 games. Yet it was a season of spectacular individual performances. Pedgrift (2), Brigden, Jenner, Thompson and RA Duncan, were all century makers. There were opening partnerships of 201 between Jenner (112) and Black (83) against Barclays Bank; 175 by Thompson (94) and Rees 89 n.o. against King's College Hospital; and 100 between FW Kettle (58) and Rees (44) against Banstead II. Pedgrift contributed to four century partnerships. Lucas, Cutter, Linnitt, JW Duncan, EG Purnell, HA Beardwell, GW Higgs, JN Eastwood and M Burt were also involved in match-winning and match-saving century partnership. But it is the bowling figures that have to be seen to be believed in an 'average' season.

Iberson 8 for 28 against O. Hollingtonians, 7 for 67 against Richmond, 6 for 28 against Dulwich, 6 for 43 against Mitcham, 6 for 53 against Sutton, 6 for 56 against Beddington; and it was only a partial season for that astonishing wrist-and-finger spinner who was pursued by several counties but was already suffering arthritic pain because of damage to the joints of his crucial spinning fingers; he was more often absent because of injury and the call of teaching duties than he was present on the cricket field. Then there was Kelsh, 8 for 39 against Spencer, 7 for 67 against Kenley, and the new player HJ Webb's 7 for 14 against Westminster Bank IV. It is a common enough saying in cricket that 'bowlers win matches' but bowlers are sometimes entitled to ask what they have to do for that axiom to be borne out in practice.

All the hopes of Wisdom's years of captaincy were to be realised in his absence in 1953. It was the club's year to head the *Evening Standard* table in the South, while Ilford, seldom far from the top, won pride of place in the North. But the trail was a hard one and not until the last few games were Beddington, the holders, and Old Whitgiftians overtaken.

In the build up, there were the customary jitters and some remarkable performances. Streatham, replying to Cyphers 114, were all out for 24; Iberson taking 8 for 7, Dorset the other two wickets. There was also an eight wicket win over Spencer, with JW Duncan scoring 121 not out and Jenner 54; and Iberson taking 7 wickets for 74. In Cricket Week, without Iberson and some other key players, it wasn't quite as easy. Kent Club and Ground with some names soon to be prominent in the Kent County side declared at 203 for 4, and bowled out the hosts for 83. The MCC match fizzled out with the visitors reaching 156 for 4 in reply to 230; Ted Purnell playing for MCC in his qualifying match was their top scorer with 72, while Black carried his bat for Cyphers with 155. Against Stoics, the club could turn out only a motley selection from lower elevens (Black was the only First XI player), but they contrived an extraordinary tie, with Stoics achieving a last-ball bye to bring the score to 216 apiece. The traditional last game against Beckenham produced a redoubtable 5 wickets victory.

In fact, Black's first season as captain was to prove one of the most successful in the club's history – not just in terms of First XI achievement which was virtually assured by its bowling strength, but in terms of the club's all-round performance throughout the five elevens and at every level. If, for example, Iberson was able to demonstrate figures of 87 maidens, 959 runs and 133 wickets from 372 overs, averaging 7.21, it remains a surprising fact that he was second to a new player, D Ballantine, who, playing in lower elevens, bowled 239 overs for 398 runs at an average of 6.86. AR Purnell (no relation to Ted, incidentally) came second in the batting averages and fourth in the bowling figures, as ever playing mostly for the 4th XI.

In the Saturday fixtures which counted towards the *Evening Standard* Challenge Match and the unofficial club championship there was no final impediment to Cyphers' reaching the winning post, though it was a close run thing: 20 matches played, 11 won, 6 drawn and only 1 lost. Precedence over Old Whitgiftians was achieved by one point; over Beddington by two. The final was at Brondesbury on Wednesday 16 September, with test umpires Frank Lee and Harry Baldwin standing. And in more ways than one, the encounter with Ilford was to prove a watershed.

'A thrilling finish showed that competitive cricket has much to commend itself', wrote the *Evening Standard* cricket reporter Dennis Roberts. In a very real sense they were words that would help to bring about the eventual demise of clubs like Cyphers, with their heavy overheads and under employed social facilities and with little hope of ever again attracting the kind of crowds that were once common at week-end cricket, willing to throw a shilling or two into the blanket that was carried hopefully by the 'early dismissals' of the home side and, together with bar takings, subs and occasional contributions from wealthy members, produced just enough income to keep the wolf from the door.

Sufficient unto the day was the event itself.

Purnell, Cyphers most in-form batsman at that time, was forced to withdraw from the side on the morning of the match when he received news of his father's death. His place was taken by David Thomas, a relatively new member.

After winning the toss, deciding to bat on a rain soaked wicket, and losing four for 59, there was little optimism in the camp. The middle order saved the day, however, and Black was able to declare at 167 for 7. Ilford were left two and a half hours to make the runs. Assisted by several dropped catches off both Iberson and Kelsh, Ilford were able to put on 127 for 4, and with 30 minutes to go were cruising to victory. Then Kelsh and Iberson performed a left-arm double act, taking alternate wickets for 3, 13, 0, 4. The scene changed completely and Cyphers gathered in menacing array round the last batsmen. Ilford's last man came in with over nine minutes go. But one of the most lethal pairs of spinners in club cricket was unable to break the last wicket resistance and Ilford forced a draw; 146 for 9. For Cyphers supporters it was a moral victory, none the less, and for a long time afterwards it was said in SE20 and Beckenham, with only slight manhandling of the truth, that Cyphers were the champions of Southern, if not English, club cricket.

The scorecard read:

CYPHERS

T Jenner lbw b Lynch	11
J Duncan c Smock b Lynch	14
L Black c Harding b Ralph	10
D Thomas b Lynch	6
N Pedgrift c Pavitt b Faragher	37
B Thompson not out	55

G Higgs lbw b Abbott..............................   19

F Kelsh c Ralph b Lynch.........................   5

Extras   10

TOTAL (for 7 wkts decl.)   <u>167</u>

F Brigden, W Dorset and J Iberson did not bat.

Bowling: Abbott 1 for 22; Lynch 4 for 34; Ralph 1 for 50; Faragher 1 for 25.

ILFORD

R Evans st Brigden b Iberson...................   70

K Harding c Thompson b Higgs...............   0

D Crown c Brigden b Iberson..................   37

R Ralph c Duncan b Kelsh......................   3

R Lynch b Kelsh....................................   5

H Faragher lbw b Kelsh..........................   3

G Smock st Brigden b Iberson.................   13

A Brooker b Kelsh.................................   0

R Pavitt b Iberson.................................   4

D Poole not out.....................................   2

G Abbott not out...................................   0

Extras...........   9

TOTAL   (for 9 wickets)   <u>146</u>

Bowling: Higgs 1 for 15; Iberson 4 for 61; Kelsh 4 for 28

To complete a year which met with all-round approval, the Second eleven under the captaincy of Eric Wadman 'capped a most successful season', to use the Committee's words, with a Sussex tour against exceptionally strong opponents in very hospitable territory. From then on the Sussex tour became a regular event in the calendar.

Cyphers was at it zenith; only the indoor bowling green that had been hit by a rocket in war remained out of action, and that was about to be restored. Neither was success confined to cricket. Extensive grass courts were occupied by a growing army of accomplished tennis players and several of the section's members represented the County. Bowls were thriving. Tulse Hill still played hockey on the front pitch in the off season and kept the pavilion bar ticking over. All seemed set fair by the winter of 1953.

5

Rise and Decline

'All seemed set fair'. The concluding phrase of the last chapter is worth repeating, for things aren't always as they seem.

'Cricket final ends in thrill', ran the *Evening Standard* headline on the day after the dramatic draw between Cyphers and Ilford in September 1953. And the President of the Club Cricket Conference, Len Newman, told the newspaper: 'There certainly has been a great deal of interest in the Evening Standard table of merit. It has brought bigger crowds to club games and this should in the long run help the clubs financially.' All remained of like mind by the ensuing season, but there were a few rumblings of discontent at the idea of competitive club cricket.

The Ilford match marked the final appearance of one of Cyphers' – indeed club cricket's – finest opening batsmen, Tom Jenner. Lbw for 11, he bowed out of the First XI and out of the game in much the way he had graced it for so many years, with quiet and dignified self effacement. At the last he was twelfth in the overall batting averages (23.12), fifth in the 1st XI's, with a mere 578 runs from 25 appearances. It is a mystery that a man who had headed the averages so often, only four times in twenty years slipping below the thirty mark, who had made his thousand runs time and again, played so little representative cricket. In all probability his profession made mid-week appearances difficult if not impossible. At any rate, he left the game as he entered it, without fuss or pretension, an opening bat whose performances week in and week out would take a lot of bettering, and replacing.

As it happened, there was stiff competition for the club's batting places, much of it from lower elevens; while bowling remained the province of two or three players at the highest level. But there was a contrary flow. Jim Wardle, whose batting had proved a power not far short of his outstanding father's, had emigrated to Canada before the Ilford final — WA, incidentally, still played for the Fourth XI and went on into his seventies. Frank Dorset married a Danish girl soon after and, though he played on and off for Cyphers for a few seasons he eventually emigrated to his wife's country and played international cricket for the Danish national side. Jimmy Black was nearing the end of his playing career.

As the Committee noted, the 1953 season had not only ended on a successful note for the First XI but also for the club in general. The First had won 14 of their 27 games, drawing 10. All teams together had won 71 of the 143 matches played, drawing 33 and losing 39. The First had 22.23 runs per wicket against the opposition's 15.32; and the club had averaged 17.62 against 13.70. Yet at times, batting looked frail.

In 1954, John Duncan (who had headed the First XI and Club batting averages the previous season), Higgs and Kelsh, were shuffled with Black for the opening places in early fixtures; then Kettle was put up the order and Rees came up from the Second XI to give further variety to the partnership with Black. Soon Wisdom, who had found some of his old form with the Seconds, returned to familiar pastures, making a top score of 37 in a low scoring victory over Westminster Bank (Iberson taking 6 for 45 and Dorset 4 for 22) in June. Whizz had been one of six ducks in a May game with the Seconds against Beddington, in a total of 81 (Rees 55), which score the opposition reached with the loss of 4 wickets. 'Batting Was Not Good Enough', said the *Journal* with a hint of understatement on 26 June when the 1st eleven had responded to Streatham's 120 on the previous Saturday with 88 all out. Wisdom was top scorer with 21.

Narrow victory over Beddington and a draw with Dulwich led up to the 1954 Cricket Week in July. In the opening fixture with Midland Bank heavy defeat was visited on a side in which the absence of regular bowlers made it necessary for Wisdom to turn an increasingly reluctant arm. All the same, he took 3 for 39 out of a total score of 251 for 8 declared. With Kelsh in the attack to claim 6 for 20, it was a different story in the contest with Stoics. The visitors were all out for 74 on a rain affected wicket, and Cyphers gained a 7 wickets victory. Decisive victory over the Wanderers and equally decisive defeat at the hands of Kent Club and Ground, and defeat by a single run scored off the last ball of their innings by Beckenham, brought a good week's cricket to a close.

Exceptional performance figures can be relied upon to fascinate any cricketer, even when he is among the victims of cutthroat bowling or imperious batting or gymnastic fielding. But there can be few examples in the long and convoluted story of cricket to compare with a match reported in the October 1954 issue of the *Alleynian*. Whizz kept a copy of the story related in his old school magazine and pasted it in his scrapbook. The match was between forms 1G and 2G, the latter containing several boys who played for the school under 14s.

The scorer tells all.

2G

Carmichael, M.N., c Kent b Fay	0
Fairbairns, D.A.W., b Mottley	0
Longhurst, .J.A., lbw b Fay	0
Sturgess, C.M., c Harker b Mottley	0
Barnett, A.P.J., b Fay	0
Haigh, R.A., b Fay	0
Chalmers, A.S., b Mottley	0
Breeze, M.J., c Bates b Mottley	0
Pearce M.J.F., lbw b Mottley	0
Curra, P.J., not out	0
White, R.S. absent	-
Byes...	1
Total	1

Bowling
Mottley 5 for 0
Fay 4 for 0

1G

Mottley, P.E.	not out	1
Harker, O.E.E.	not out	0

Bates, D.H.T., Fay, D.A.,
Farrow, G.M., Curwin, R.N.,
Wicks, D.J., Kent, D.A., Reed, C.J.,
Langford, C.R.E., Gordon, P.A.J., did not bat

Byes	1
Total (for no wicket)	2

Back to Cyphers in 1954. The importance of Iberson, who had been missing for all but the Beckenham game in Cricket Week, was soon apparent when the normal Saturday programme resumed in August. In the Streatham match he took 8 for 34 to pave the way to an easy win.

There were other exceptional bowling performances in which Kelsh and Dorset shared most of the honours with Ibers. As the season approached its end, however, the club's batting was going through a crisis familiar to any club with its normal share of human frailty. Black was going through a bad patch, and opening partnerships were being shared by GW Higgs, John Duncan, FW Kettle and Frank Kelsh, with Black going in at three or four. Wicket-keeper Ken Moore, Wisdom and Purnell were among the higher scoring bats. But the end-of-season averages, headed by Higgs with 29.75, were an indication of a far from satisfactory overall performance. Black's captaincy had coincided with an obvious loss of form and he handed over in the following season to the club's most experienced and widely respected all-rounder, Kelsh. The decision was soon vindicated.

'Good Century by Purnell' was the local paper's tribute to a handsome contribution (122) to Cyphers score of 265 for 5 decl. against Beckenham in the first match of the 1955 season. A rejuvenated Black opened with 70 and partnered Purnell in a stand of 127 for the second wicket. Iberson took 5 for 48 and Kelsh 3 for 46 as Beckenham just held out with 182 for 9 wickets. And there was an even better resolution to the next match at Banstead where the home side's 152 was passed for the loss of only three wickets, Black and Purnell again scoring most of the runs. The *News Chronicle* sent a sports reporter[1] to Sutton's fixture with Cyphers in the second week of May. In fact, the home club's new pavilion, which qualified them for a Minor Counties' game in the summer, caused other organs of the national press to take notice too, but Fleet Street's news hounds were not detained for any length of time. Sutton were bowled out by Higgs and newcomer Paul Clark for 74. After losing the first four wickets for 28, Duncan and Peter Smith, the latter recently promoted from the Second XI, saw Cyphers safely home. Narrowly contrived draws with Streatham and Dulwich followed, before a three-wicket victory against perhaps the strongest of local opposition, Beddington, restored the optimism of the season's opening weeks. Another century from Purnell (109) was the highlight of Cyphers' innings of 227 for 7.

It was, however, an administrative rather than a playing matter that caused the biggest stir in club circles as high summer approached. A circular to members from the Club Cricket Conference asked them all to withdraw their names from the league tables published regularly throughout the season by the

---

[1] Doug Ibbertson

Evening Standard. 'CONFERENCE WANT TO STOP CLUB CRICKET TABLE', ran the new headline. It was a charge that would remain at the heart of club cricket debate and controversy for years to come. The CCC letter stressed that 'although...no Conference rules have been broken, the table and challenge matches might eventually lead to an attitude not in accordance with the professed aims of the Conference'. Mike Murray the Beddington skipper, Vic Ransom of Malden Wanderers, Tony Fairbairns of Dulwich, all publicly opposed the CCC position. Of the reigning 'champions', Cyphers captain Frank Kelsh, like his Ilford counterpart, remained silent. The *Evening Standard* meanwhile published the current table. It showed Hounslow, Wanstead, Kenton, Chingford, Hampton Wick and Alexandra Palace occupying the top positions in the North; Beddington, Cyphers, Sutton, Private Banks, Bromley and Catford in the South. But it was only 6 July.

Four wins in six games marked the long hot days of Cricket Week. Of the two defeats, one was inflicted by an MCC side captained by Purnell who, following his election in the previous year, brought the first of several teams from HQ to Kings Hall Road. At one stage Cyphers were 3 for 3 in reply to MCC's 240 before two guest players, SE Coles and KR Dodd restored substance to the batting with a century partnership. It wasn't enough to save the game however. The other defeat was at the hands of Kent C&G. In the Beckenham match, Wisdom (100), Higgs (47), Purnell (54) were the major contributors to a score of 267 for 4 decl. The opposition were bowled out for 193, Iberson taking 8 for 93.

Whether or not the CCC approved, Saturday fixtures had become *de facto* league engagements. Cyphers and Beddington were battling for top place in the South table, with Private Banks, O. Alleynians and O. Whitgiftians close behind. But unexpected defeats by NatProv, Spencer and Gravesend ended the hope of a second *Evening Standard* final for the club. There was another spectacular conquest for Iberson before the season was over. In the September game against O. Whifgiftians he took 7 for 50, including the wicket of R Subba Row who was on leave from his County side, Northants, for whom he had scored 260 not out against Lancs in the previous July. In the Cyphers match at Croydon, Ibers took six wickets for 55. Beddington and Hounslow were the eventual finalists in the *Evening Standard* competition.

The Cricket Section report for the 1955 season looked back and forth with mixed feelings of joy and trepidation. In terms of climate – often the cricketer's most persistent enemy – 1955 compared favourably with the glorious summers of 1947 and 1949, or so the Committee insisted. 'Unlike most of the calamities that befall the English nation', the weather could not however be said to have contributed to 'the troubles of the club'. A warning that had gone out from the Conference to affiliated clubs during the season was now echoing in the pavilions of the clubs themselves. Membership was dropping off. Playing strength was diminishing in the lower elevens which were the guarantors of senior success in future years. The First eleven had acquitted itself well. But the Seconds had not enjoyed 'their customary success' and the three lower elevens had recorded just 17 wins between them, against 28 defeats. 'It is obvious that trends have developed for which reasons must be sought', said the report. As always when the matter of club strength is discussed among sportsmen, the conclusion is inevitable if not always palatable. Some members are unhappy and seek their weekend pleasures elsewhere; others find more receptive outlets for their particular talents.

A fear never far from the surface at this time, however, was the anticipated impact of league competition on a game whose entire history and deepest traditions were based on the concept of unselfish sportsmanship. Vainglory and public acclaim had no part in a game founded on the precepts of Sir Henry Newbolt, as far as most of its older players and administrators were concerned. But a brasher generation schooled in war was beginning to tread the sacred turf, and it would not be long before comprehensive education and the demise of the grammar school became apparent on the field of play. Things were changing and there was understandable concern in the air. Cyphers playing membership had declined by a dozen in the course of the year.

Praise was loud for the First eleven's leading batsman Ted Purnell who had taken over from John Duncan with an average of more than forty, two of the club's five recorded centuries, and an aggregate just short of 1,000. But only four other bats had exceeded 500 — Bills, wicket keeper Ken Moore, Wisdom, and Peter Rees. Jimmy Bills had come back to cricket and something like his old form after a long period of illness and personal problems; 'a salutary example' in the Committee's words. David Stott, playing chiefly for the Second eleven as a recognised and elegant bat, headed the bowling figures for the second year running. The previous year he had bowled just enough overs to qualify for inclusion. This time he bowled 32 overs for 96, with five maidens and 14 wickets, to average 6.86. The figures could not be gainsaid, though they seemed only to underline the illustrious performances of Iberson. Season after season his figures for Cyphers – and for the many representative sides who risked chaotic changes in the batting order so as to accommodate his late arrival on a delayed bus – were little short of staggering. His 519 overs for 1536 runs, 105 maidens, produced 150 wickets in 1955, and an average of 10.24. Such figures in any grade of cricket are reserved for bowlers of exemplary class. As the report put it: 'This year his figures are, if possible, even more imposing than ever. There is something of special note in almost every aspect of his final analysis'. His 9 for 9 against Westminster Bank was an unneighbourly contribution to the August Bank Holiday, and the best match analysis of the season.

The decade of the 'fifties was still embroiled in the aftermath of war, and national service still took its toll of sports club membership. 1956 also suffered from appalling weather, a repetition of the 1954 season's downpours, with three entire weekends washed out. One way and another it was a lean time for the club. And if there was a tendency to blame the inclement weather, the Committee was at pains to point out that the excuse 'should apply equally to all clubs'.

It was a long and depressing report that greeted the last of Kelsh's three seasons of captaincy, for that fine all-round cricketer had decided that he too was nearing the end of his playing days. The Club's overall record was in substantial deficit for the first time since 1945. Of 130 matches played, 53 were lost, 46 won and 31 drawn.

The First XI's record was better than average, 7 won and 8 lost out of 25 matches. There were some notable partnerships: 151 for the 2nd wicket by Black and Smith v Spencer, 137 for the 1st wicket by Duncan and Stott v Northern Assurance, 134 for the 4th wicket by Purnell and Pedgrift v Lloyds Bank, 124 for 1st wicket by Rees and Black against Banstead, and 111 for the 4th by KM

Dodd and Ken Moore against WA Davidson's XI in Cricket Week. Black, Purnell, Duncan and Moore – in that order – topped the batting averages, but only Black exceeded 30.

Surprisingly, John Iberson was relegated to third place in the bowling figures with a mere 9.81 average from 424 overs which permitted 1109 runs and secured 113 wickets. Arthur Faulkner and Wally Letchford, both playing for a revitalised 4th XI under a new captain, Ted Gregory, had averages of 7.79 and 7.93 respectively. The performance of keeper-batsman Ken Moore behind the stumps deserves particular notice. He had taken over from FE Brigden as the 1st XI's regular keeper in 1955 after performing to a very high standard in the Seconds. In truth, he was the only Cyphers keeper who could genuinely 'read' Iberson, though just to make sure what was coming up next a code was established between them. Ibers would flick his left ear as he walked back to his bowling mark when he was to deliver the googly, or his right ear for the chinaman. But it was largely an unnecessary refinement. Moore could follow his wrist and body action perfectly and in most seasons after the mid-fifties he topped the club dismissals table. In 1956 he was instrumental in sending back 46 opponents, 26 caught, 30 stumped, mostly off Iberson.

It was the end of Kelsh's brief reign as captain, though his much longer reign as one of the south-east of England's finest all-rounders would survive for some time to come. It was also the end of Rupert Holloway's intimate association with the Club. In March his 25 years of day-to-day association with the Cyphers CC came officially to an end when he relinquished the chairmanship of the section, though he remained President of the Club and took on the new title of Life Patron. He had served the CCC as member, player, chairman and president since the end of the war and of course the Conference was represented at a farewell dinner at King's Hall Road. Andy Sandham and Laurie Fishlock were there too, along with representatives of Beckenham, Streatham, Old Whitgiftians and Beddington. Eric Wadman, 'Waddy', proposed a toast at the pavilion party given in Rupert's honour, recounting some of his many achievements as bat and fielder. He was indeed one of the best fielders in the game, a product of the athleticism that had made him an amateur international footballer at the age of 17. Nothing quite compared with his bowling feat in an MCC game in 1935, however.

> The Hon. Remnant had scored 159. The Captain of Cyphers put Rupert Holloway on to bowl - and Remnant was out, caught and bowled with his first ball.

It must have been the first time the man who was always referred to deferentially as 'Mr Holloway' was allowed to bowl when the batting was on top.

Ted Purnell, taking over the captaincy from Frank Kelsh, made the presentation of a silver salver to the retiring chairman.

The new skipper made a good start to the 1957 season. 'Purnell hits 130 in drawn game', was the headline that greeted the opening game against Beckenham. For the moment, the batting line up had a more or less familiar look – Rees, Kelsh, Purnell, Pedgrift, Higgs – but there were new faces on the scene and the old spearhead had begun to show signs of wear. Jimmy Black gave up at last. John Duncan, who played his first game for the club as a 15-year-old schoolboy in 1937, a regular and at times prolific higher order bat since the early 'fifties, had become a more or less regular Second XI opener.

A disastrous Cricket Week in July underlined growing problems in the higher batting echelons. Defeats at the hands of Midland Bank (by 7 wickets), the Wanderers (9 wickets), Purnell's MCC (8 wickets), all matches from which Iberson was absent, were clear indications of a decline in batting and an imbalance in bowling that would add up to a dismal statistical picture in the end of season report — Played 30, Won 7, Lost 13, Drawn 10. Second XI figures were almost identical, with one less played and one less drawn; Third and Fourth XIs about the same, given fewer matches played. All in all: P147, W44, L60, D43.

A new Third eleven bat, KP Fenton, topped the batting averages at 35.18, less than one run ahead of Purnell at 34.78. After that it was Beardwell, HA; Kelsh, FJ; Rees, P; Pedgrift, NF; Wadman, WE; Wisdom, EM; to name but the first eight. Only one new name. That was the Committee's chief bone of contention when it came to chew over the season's work. Purnell's 130 against Beckenham, Beardwell's 121 against Streatham II, Rees's 117 not against Bickley Park, and another new name, N Dolder's 114 not against Old Colfeians 'B', were highlights of the season's batting and there were further centuries from Pedgrift, Purnell, Beardwell and Wisdom, but they weren't enough to change the overall direction of the club's performance, downward. It was a different story on the bowling front — Iberson, alone and inevitably, at the top of the table, 118 wickets from 490 overs, 118 maidens, 1245 runs, ave. 10.55. Jack Guest – who had been around since the immediate aftermath of the war, a medium pace bowler who never went anywhere without his cricket gear lest someone was a man short – came next with 15.2. Then PB Clark (15.12), consistent as a bat and a fast-medium supplement to Kelsh and Iberson in the club's front-line attack, was third[2], and perhaps the most colourful recent addition to Cyphers' playing ranks, WW Gaylarde (15.86), fourth.

The moment for a significant drawing of breath had arrived. The Committee report for 1956, it will be recalled, had complained at length about the declining membership of the club, a decline that had affected its batting strength in particular. It also reflected on the club's continuing ability to field five Saturday elevens, and often three on Sundays. The official word could hardly have been more emphatic.

> In this situation, the Committee is certain that it will not be possible to field five Saturday elevens in the 1957 season unless new members are forthcoming. Moreover, to forestall any contention that our troubles could be cured by dispensing with the 5th XI, the Committee must point out that, apart from the serious financial blow to the Section and to the Club that this would represent, the decline in playing strength has affected us in quality as well as in quantity. If the Club fails to attract a flow of new players of maturity and competence, as well as the desirable influx of young and promising members, we shall run a definite risk of forfeiting our place in the top rank of London clubs, especially if we are obliged to cut down from five sides to four.

There was another concern too.

> Moreover, in common with all other sections, the Cricket Section has been called upon by the Executive Committee to achieve a substantial increase in its contribution to Club finances next year. This is not a matter of convenience: it is a sheer necessity.

---

[2] To confuse the picture, another new all-rounder in the club was PJB Clark, and they were soon joined by Ezra Clark(e) and Cyril 'Cy' Clark(e)!

The report went on to an argument familiar to anyone who has ever served on the committee of a sports club — should subs go up, should food and bar prices be increased, should indirect methods of fund raising be employed? As most committee men and women will concede, the one thing no one in such a situation is ever prepared to consider is the possibility that the organisation might change its ways to accommodate a changing world. At Cyphers, as at so many other distinguished sports clubs near and far, the inclination was to 'stay as we are', in tennis and bowls as well as cricket. In many ways, attitudes that had hardened in the Wardle affair more than twenty years earlier, had come home to roost. Allied to the ongoing question of league cricket and the desirability of competition taking over in a 'gentleman's' world, all the elements were in place for a long struggle for survival. But the crunch was not quite imminent. There was still hope, especially for the Fifth XI, in the shape of the new skipper, WW 'Bill' Gaylarde, one of the club's truly memorable characters, and his 'vice', Eric Allen. There would be no 'Fifth' in 1957, however.

Things did not improve in 1958. Played 30, won 7, lost 12, drawn 11. Again, the First XI reflected Club performance with uncanny accuracy — played 151, won 46, lost 63, drawn 42. Batting was reinforced by some new and highly promising talents, most of all Glen Neil-Dwyer (28) and Brian Barnett (24), second and third respectively in the averages beneath Purnell (36); a little further down the list, BH Seale and RW Collins, eighth and ninth in order. The 141 run partnership between Purnell and Neil-Dwyer for the 3rd wicket against Richmond, stood out, as did 109 for the 5th wicket against the Wanderers in Cricket Week, moved incidentally from July to August in the hope of attracting stronger players during the school holidays.[3] With the rarity of an iceberg in the Red Sea, a newly sprung left-arm spin bowler, RC De Berry, came to topple Ibers from the headship of the bowling averages, a position the latter had occupied as of right for a good many years; admittedly by 0.23 of a run. Other new and unheralded names followed in the bowling honours: Scott, Stevens, Fleet, Guest, Thomas, Rand, Sprackling, Petchey. There was renewed hope but no room for complacency at season's end.

Batting strength that had been lying somewhat dormant in the lower elevens, emerged in 1959 to give a fillip to the First XI which at last showed signs of regaining respectability if not its past position as a premier club side. And the revival was marked by some significant leadership changes. Howard Beardwell, whose connections with the club through family and self were both primordial and geographical (he joined at the age of 12, moved to a house alongside the ground and already, in his 30s, had arranged to have his remains strewn on it), took over the chairmanship from Frank Kelsh. John Iberson, after many unsuccessful attempts to persuade him to stand for election, was induced to offer himself and he became the somewhat reluctant vice-captain of the First team. In fact, 1959 and 1960 stood together as a watershed that would send the club into the 60s and its own 70th anniversary with a freshly endowed make-up, on and off the field.

An early innovation under the new regime was the Cyphers Schools Cricket Trophy, which local schools competed for keenly during the next decade. Some remember a youngster by the name of Underwood taking part for Beckenham and Penge Grammar.

---

[3] From 1957. Annual report 1956.

Others who took part as schoolboys would become well-known at King's Hall Road; and the names of 'Chalky' White, John Noakes and John Pannett spring to mind.

In 1959 the basic facts and figures were as follows:

XI	Played	Won	Lost	Drawn	Abnd
Ist	34	10	8	13	3
2nd	27	7	9	9	2
3rd	22	7	9	4	2
4th	20	2	10	7	1
5th	15	6	5	3	1
Sunday A	22	7	6	8	1
Sunday B	22	5	13	2	2
Sunday C	8	2	3	2	1
Others	4	2	1		1
	174	48	64	48	14

Century batting partnerships:

135 for 5th wicket JD Brown & BA Cheetham v Bickley
127 for 2nd R Rees & G Neil-Dwyer v Sutton
117 for 2nd J Anderson & WE Wadman v Gravesend
131 for 2nd EM Wisdom & WE Wadman v Alexandra Pk
115 for 1st EG Purnell & C Matten v Richmond

Bowling:

	Overs	Mdns	Runs	Wkts	Ave
D Neale	35	7	68	10	6.80
W Hack	66	10	223	22	10.13
J Iberson	638	140	1659	159	10.43

R Hobson	150	25	334	30	11.12
P Duncan	68	11	172	13	13.23
B Barnett	36	8	139	10	13.90

Denis Neale was a recognised keeper-batsman who had clearly abandoned gloves and pads at some stage and demonstrated that he could bowl to some effect. Even with the modest turnover of 35 overs in lower eleven cricket, 6.80 must be accounted an unusually good average. Only two players in the first six, Iberson and Barnett, had ever before appeared in the top half of the averages. All the same, it was Iberson whose record stood almost monotonously apart — 10 for 80 against Honor Oak, 8 for 52 against Norwood, 8 for 86 Midland Bank, 7 for 52 Old Roan, and so it went on.

The 1960 picture was even better as far as the Saturday elevens were concerned, though results of the Second XI and a weakened Sunday B XI adversely affected the overall picture.

XI	Played	Won	Lost	Drawn
Ist	30	13	8	9
2nd	30	8	11	11
3rd	21	11	7	3
4th	19	8	8	3
5th	8	3	4	1
Sunday A	22	11	6	5
Sunday B	22	2	17	3
Sunday C	4	2	2	
	156	58	63	35

Familiar names from the past joined with new blood in the
'notable' batting performances reported to the AGM. David Stott,
captaining and opening for the Seconds with popularity and zeal
but having to contribute his batting to a depleted First XI every
now and again, joined with Brian Cheetham to produce the best
partnership of the year, 140 for the first wicket against NatProv;
Stott 94 not out.

Dolder (still doing army service and only available for six
games in the season) and Matten added significantly to Cyphers'
batting strength. Both recruits came from St Dunstan's where the
cricket coach Billy Ibadullah was providing top-class material and
whence a number of Cyphers recruits were drawn in the wake of
their economics master's achievements[4]. Neville Dolder and Peter
Rees put on 139 for the 4th wicket against Pakistani Wanderers;
Colin Matten and Purnell 134 for the 1st against Finchley;
Wisdom and B.Roden 123 for the 3rd against Gravesend; John
Anderson and Tommy Tomkins 120 for the 1st against Spencer V;
Purnell and J Flower 110 for the 2nd against Harvey; K Miebs and
Dennis Weaver 108 for the 6th v Spencer III, Kelsh and Peter
Smith 103 for the 2nd v Barclays Bank; Purnell and Matten 101
for the 1st against Spencer; Purnell and J Rana 100 for the 1st v
the Wanderers in Cricket Week. Despite his own protestations of
incompetence, Iberson demonstrated not for the first time that he
could bat with the next when he put his mind to it. He was fourth
in order of precedence, with a top score of 27 not out from 12
innings and an average of 31.50. Wisdom, the highest aggregate
scorer in the club's history, came just behind him. In order, the

---

[4] I rely on memory in naming St Dunstans' old boys, and in describing John
Iberson's academic subject. Author

averages read Matten, Kelsh, Purnell, Iberson, Wisdom, Neil-Dwyer, Miebs, Moore, Stott, Seale, Barnett, Flower, to name a richly assorted dozen. Bowling, equally, was a mixture of familiar and new names. The 1st XI report for the year remarked that 'No less than four quickish bowlers of 1st team class joined the club during 1960. These were JE Flower, BP Gamble, J Rana and DNC Wood. All showed very good results with the ball and Flower and Rana also batted well'. In the club averages, Andy Davie superseded Iberson with an average of 6.69 from 75 overs against 8.97 from 609 overs; then Dennis Weaver, Jack Guest, Arthur Faulkner, Tony Stevens; Wood D, Constantine E, Duncan P, Gaylarde W. But again it was Iberson who dominated the performance tables with figures of magical proportions against the best of First XI opposition. 'The greatest single factor in the winning of games was again J. Iberson's bowling', said the report. It added that 'probably his best performance was 9 for 31 in 24 overs against the Whitgiftians — not exactly a weak batting side at any time and on this occasion including R Subba Row'. Skipper Ted Purnell tended to favour the old adage 'bowlers win matches', but in 1960 it was 'catches win matches'. He commented: 'Contributing greatly to the success of the side was the improved catching close to the wicket and those mainly responsible were Matten, Neil-Dwyer and RW Collins'.

In August, Ibers had made an extremely successful debut for Hertfordshire in the Minor Counties League, while Colin Matten did likewise for the CCC.

If 1960 was for those at the very top level of the game the year of the 'Trinidad bottle party', for mere mortals at the more modest club level it was the year when another event, just as critical in its way, threatened. An *Evening Standard* headline set the tone:

View from war damaged pavilion, 18th June 1948. Cyphers v WA Davidson's XI in Cricket Week

Unveiling of war memorial plaque, 28th September 1947, by Mayor of Beckenham,
Ald JH Atkins, with Mayor's Chaplain, Rev WJ Berry and Rupert Holloway.

Below: Members and friends at ceremony in pavilion.

Skipper EM Wisdom greets actor and MCC player Trevor Howard in Cricket Week 1951.

Below: The two teams, PBH May in front row with MCC captain WA Davidson and some Cyphers stalwarts.

Above, captain and heir presumptive. Wisdom and Purnell, v Stoics, July 1949

Below, First XI, 1952: Back row l to r: F Margham (umpire), FW Kettle, WA Dorset, PB Smith, J Iberson, EG Purnell, NF Pedgrift,
Front: TH Jenner, FJ Kelsh, EM Wisdom (Capt), FE Brigden, GW Higgs

Above, Second XI, 1953; back, R Hicks (ump), J Newton, P Smith, J Fleet, PB Clark, HA Beardwell, K Moore, FW Kettle, (front) FJ Ridout, WE Wadman, EM Wisdom, W Parker, Jean Swanton (scorer).

Below: First XI, 1966; O Small, C Matten, R Phillips, EM Wisdom, J Iberson, E Clark, B Barnett   (front), P Rees, R Collins, EG Purnell (capt), GW Higgs

Welcoming the Dutchmen, Sparta of Rotterdam, to King's Hall Road, June 1961.
Cartoon by Syd Jordan
Courtesy Kentish Times

Cyphers and Ilford, unofficial Club Champions, before the final of the Evening Standard League Trophy at Brondesbury, 16th September 1953

Sussex tourists, 1957: Back: DCC Stott, RC De Berry, J Cair, HA Beardwell, W Russell.
Middle: C Mote (umpire), J Guest, FW Parker, WE Wadman (Capt), APM Severn, EM Wisdom.
Front: A Faulkner, A Stevens

Below: *Last of the Summer Wine* or *Three Wise Men* : l to r WW 'Bill' Gaylarde,
Jack 'Curly' Cair, HJ 'Tommy' Tomkins, in last days at King's Hall Road

'Club Cricket Diehards Get a Body Blow – League fixtures are on the way'. The article beneath reported 'Twelve leading clubs in the Home Counties are already re-arranging their fixture lists with a view to starting league cricket in three years' time'.[5] Cyphers certainly was not one of the twelve. The 'open' secret was divulged at a Malden Wanderers' dinner by the club's captain Keith Walker. Vic Ransom, former Malden and Surrey II captain, supported the scheme, saying that if the game wasn't given a 'shot in the arm, club cricket as we have known it is doomed'.

As the 1961 season got under way, the big news in North Kent was that the County side failed by only 7 runs to register its first defeat of the Australian tourists since 1889; and that Cyphers had reinstated its pre-war fixture with the Dutch cricket authorities. Unfortunately the old opponents, Flemingos, had gone out of business with the war and the visitors this time were the Rotterdam side Sparta.

In fact, the year's achievements made less than encouraging reading at season's end, despite a whole series of outstanding individual performances right through the elevens. Constantine, related incidentally to one of the greatest of all cricketers, Sir Leary, made 150 not out against Elmers End, a pre-war fixture that had been revived in 1959. Brown, a player who had distinguished himself in the 'glorious 5th', a side for which he preferred to play, made 147 against Kenley. Matten (2), Purnell, Dick Ballam and Stott were all century makers. Wisdom, playing for the 3rd, 4th and 5th elevens with unabated zest ended the season back in a familiar position among the averages, second at 35.09, a fraction below David Stott at the head of the table.

---

[5] *Evening Standard*, Dec 18, 1960

Another new player, Jim Roberts, was third, followed by Matten, Purnell and John Anderson, the latter also among those who was happy to play for any of the five sides and who seemed to do well with scornful indifference to the strength of the opposition. The 211 for the 4th wicket between Brown and Purnell against Kenley was by far the best of the year's partnerships. There were several century partnerships for the first wicket worthy of note: 152 by Brooker and Stott v Steyning; 151 by Constantine and Barnett v Elmers End; 137 by Barnett and Ballam v Spencer, 127 by Matten and Purnell v Honor Oak; 123 by Anderson and Matten v Christchurch. On the closing day of the season, the drawn Cyphers v Dulwich match made national headlines with another remarkable solo performance by Iberson, 7 for 59, and an even more remarkable wicket-keeping performance by Ken Moore who made a record six stumpings, five of them off Ibers. The first-class record at that time was six, achieved by Yarnold for Worcester against Scotland in 1951.[6] And in an orgy of coincidence Cyphers' senior sides on both Saturday and Sunday, 23 and 24 September, were set targets of 138 by Dulwich and Richmond, and on each occasion the club scored 118 for nine to force the draw.[7] But when all was said and done, the First eleven had played 32, won 9, lost 12, drawn 11, and had scored 4874 runs against the opposition's combined figure of 5244. Other sides performed comparably, though the Third eleven enjoyed a credit balance of two victories and scored more runs than the opposition.

First eleven results overall were still in the doldrums by the end of the 1962 season — 13 lost, 9 won and 7 drawn out of the 29

---

[6] *Evening News,* Tuesday, 26 September, 1961.

[7] *Advertiser*, Thursday, 28 September, 1961

games played. But there were distinct signs of progress lower down. The Second team under David Stott's leadership won 9 and lost 6 of its 22 matches. Stott had led from the front since he took over three years earlier; he was a consistent performer with the bat (ably assisted by his vice Dick Ballam who was one of the most resolute bats in the club), and he, Stott, featured in the best partnership of the year, 144 with John Duncan for the fourth wicket against Old Alleynians. But it was the Third, Fourth and Fifth elevens that exceeded their seniors' performances and all expectations with margins of victory that gave the club a welcome score of 65 wins against 51 defeats with 49 draws from 165 fixtures. The new all-round success doubtless owed something to new blood that had been around since the late 'fifties and had by the early 'sixties produced outstanding players at all levels and two of the club's most individualistic skippers, Denis Neale of the Third and Bill Gaylarde of the Fifth.

Neale, schoolmaster and stoic cricketer, led his side to several years of ascendancy over its established opposition, with captaincy based largely on the proposition that 'a happy team is a good team' and a sizeable playing contribution as wicket keeper/batsman who, as we have seen, could bowl if the mood was upon him. He took over the captaincy from the inimitable Jack 'Curly' Cair, whose large frame, nagging off-breaks and sparse hair were renowned in about equal measure through the late '50s and the '60s.

Gaylarde, the great eccentric of Cyphers' post-war history, was a one off; a salesman who preferred to be known by the traditional term 'commercial traveller', whose motor car was always occupied by a vast array of ladies' and gents' garments of every description, an assortment of much-used cricket gear, and a fiercely protective dog. He, Gaylarde, was an artful off-spinner who had learnt his trade in the African colonies to which he was despatched after leaving Clifton school and where, on matting wickets, he learnt to mesmerise batsmen of every degree. He also acquired there the habit of speaking to his fellow men with a directness and lack of finesse that opposition skippers were liable to interpret as a declaration of war. It was only after several seasons of his unique brand of captaincy that the 'glorious Fifth' came to be understood, then accepted and ultimately welcomed wherever they went. Because there was not always a sufficient pool of members available on a Saturday, the Fifth was allowed to invite outsiders and thus became the club's unofficial recruitment centre; and it was through the 5th that the likes of Brown, Barnett, Neale, Cummings and many other players and would-be players, including – dare it be said? – the present writer, were introduced to the club. In the previous season Brown had shared with Purnell in a fourth wicket partnership that produced 211, of which his share was 147. He preferred to play for the 5th, however, and in the 1962 season, he had made two scores of 96 not out for Gaylarde's warriors – arousing some suspicion among the opposition by the fluency of his stroke play – and had gone on to score a robust 84 against John Iberson's XI in a Sunday fixture. RW Collins (42.40), Matten (39.00), Ballam (37.09) and Brown (31.08) headed a new-look batting averages table, with Purnell relegated to an uncommon seventh place with 25.83. Bowling too had an unfamiliar look: P Gilmour (7.36), R Sloss (9.10), A Faulkner (10.02), J Iberson (11.00). D Gaffney, B Barnett, J Guest and W Gaylarde were among old and new practitioners of the noble art in close attendance. The 'Dismissals' column offers an insight into the club's wicket-keeping riches at this time, with several occasional keepers only too willing to put on gloves and pads when the opportunity offered: Moore (still the only keeper who could read Iberson with anything like assurance), 26 stumped, 17 caught; APM Severn, keeper-captain of the Fourth, 16 stumped, 21 caught; W Russell, Second XI, 9 stumped, 24 caught; E Constantine, deputising, 10 stumped, 18 caught; D. Neale, Third XI, 7 stumped, 12 caught; V Scully, Fifth XI, 7 stumped, 12 caught; Barnett, deputising, 1 stumped, 16 caught; J Rand, deputising, 2 stumped, 13 caught; K Letchford, deputising, 1 stumped, 11 caught; R Jones, deputising, 2 stumped, 9 caught; K Ford, deputising, 4 stumped, 5 caught. At the AGM Rupert Holloway proudly proclaimed that the club was back to its pre-war position as 'one of the premier clubs in the South of England'.[8]

It would be churlish to conclude an account of 1962 without reference yet again to Iberson's representative achievements. Chosen for the Minor Counties against the Pakistani tourists in August, he claimed the wickets of Mushtaq Mohammad and Shahid Mahmood in the first innings, ending with an analysis of 2 for 44 in 14 overs. In a game that ended in a draw, with the tourists set to score 82 in 40 minutes in their second innings, it was no surprise that spin was forsaken for the speed of SH Young and Peter Lever as Inthikab failed by seven runs to meet the challenge. Few doubted after that display, however, that Ibers could hold his own in the most distinguished company. He took 15 wickets for Herts in the season, as well as his 96 for the club, making an aggregate to date of 1,250 wickets. In the same month, Cricket Week at King's Hall Road was all but washed out by the

---

[8] *Kentish Times,* 14 December 1962

rain. In one completed match against Old Alleynians, Brian Barnett made 62 against his own 'old boys' out of a total of 192. Alleynians knocked off the runs for 5 wickets. And to complete a season of mixed fortune, all Cyphers sides ended the week-end of 18/19 August unbeaten. Among famous victories and staunch rearguard actions, nothing was more pleasing that the 81 impeccable runs scored by Brooker in a 71 run victory over Midland Bank. Alan Brooker had recently returned to the game after a serious illness two years before which, at the time, seemed likely to put a premature end to an excellent batting prospect.

Purnell's five years of captaincy so far had been a personal triumph but a period of mixed fortune for his team. What looked like a favourable turn round in 1959 and 1960 had given way to a lean '61 and '62 in which losses in both years significantly outweighed successful outcomes. As the skipper made abundantly clear in his annual reports over this period, much depended on the availability of Iberson. The club's batting strength was formidable by 1963. Matten had by now become the Firsts' regular opener and most elegant batsman, and had played with distinction for the Conference and Surrey Seconds. But he was closely trailed in the batting figures by Purnell, Collins, the newcomer Cyril Clarke, Bob Phillips, and Barnett. And several players in the 2nd and 3rd elevens – the likes of Stott, Ballam, Peter Smith, Constantine – were quite capable of making plenty of runs in the First. Bowling, however, was mightily dependent on Iberson, especially when turning wickets were on offer. When he was called away to play for Herts, Stoics, the Wanderers or the Conference, as happened frequently in the 1960s, team performance suffered noticeably. But half way through the 1963 season, another player of West Indian pedigree joined the club (Constantine having made his mark over several seasons). His name was Small and he had the initials 'OR' though he was always known at the club as Neill. He was an all-rounder who was said to be related to England pace bowler Gladstone Small[9] and to have played for his native Barbados. The two men certainly bore an uncanny physiognomic likeness to each other, and their physiques and bowling actions were remarkably similar. Neill struck terror into the hearts of a good many top-class club batsmen as they became aware of his reputation, speed and aggression. In combination with Iberson he brought a lethal quality to Cyphers' bowling, added significantly to already high quality of the batting, and provided a close fielding capacity that would have graced any county stage. Indeed, it wasn't long before several counties showed an interest in the newcomer.

Cyphers were not alone at this time in discovering exceptional bowling talents. Neighbours Beckenham had a schoolboy left-arm bowler by the name of Derek Underwood who at the beginning of May had been given an outing with the full Kent XI, and the *Daily Express* decided to send its special cricket reporter Keith Miller to Foxgrove Road to have a look at him. The headline that followed, 'Underwood is a Wow', augured well for Beckenham if not for English usage or the opposition.

Miller's report said:

> '17 year-old Derek Underwood is one of the best English teenagers I have seen in years... His best delivery was the slow one which he held back with the cunning of a veteran. This, I think,

---

[9] I remember hearing this on good authority but have not checked it. *Author*

will be his main wicket taker... Oddly enough, he bowls most of his
deliveries round the wicket to left- and right-handed batsmen.'[10]

It was a method of bowling that Cyphers batsmen had encountered
already and which would help to make the bowling strengths of
Beckenham's two senior clubs more combative than any in the
South of England, outside of the first-class game.

As for Cyphers' new recruit, Small, he finished the season fifth
in the batting averages at a modest 22.66 from 25 innings. Matten,
Stott, Ballam and Smith were above him but of those only Matten
was a regular First eleven player. He could only manage 16th pace
in the bowling figures but, again, of those above him only two,
Cyril Clarke and Bob Phillips, were regular selections for the
First. It was not a sensational entrance by Small, but his 127,
including a partnership of 151 with Collins for the 5th wicket,
against Gravesend was a pointer to things to come; so was his 7
for 62 against Westminster Bank.

End-of season figures bore out the new strength of the First
team, Won 11, Lost 6, Drawn 10. Lower down the elevens the
picture was less decisive, the Second losing 9 against 7 wins,
Third and Fifth balancing out, and the Fourth claiming 8 wins
against 5 losses. Altogether the club came out on top with figures
of Played 164, Won 64, Lost 57, Drawn 42. The tide had turned,
and as if to underline Cyphers' latest renaissance, Rupert
Holloway was snatched from semi-retirement as the club's Hon.
Life Patron and elected President of the Club Cricket Conference
for 1964. At the 1962 AGM, Rupert had said that Cyphers had
'regained its prestige'. His confidence appeared to be justified.

---

[10] *Daily Express*, Monday 20th May 1963

The 1964 season showed even more emphatically the solid basis of the side's success. 'The main architects of victory were usually Iberson and Small. They bowled to their own high standards whenever they played and the club is very fortunate in possessing two bowlers so much above the average', wrote Purnell in his end-of-season report. He commented that the highest score made against the side when both were playing was the 145 made by Westminster Bank. It was no surprise that the services of both players had to be shared with representative sides, Small being required by the Conference, the Association of Kent Cricket Clubs and Kent Seconds, Iberson by Hertfordshire. As if that combination was not enough, Cyril Clarke's off spin, as in the previous season, had proved highly effective, 24 wickets at 14.9 apiece, and in Iberson's absence yet another top line bowler in MA Sweetman had appeared, taking five wickets against both Sutton and Gravesend. Purnell was a demanding captain and he was not given to unqualified approval of his men; or of himself, if the annual reports are anything of a guide There was never an admission of even the most modest achievement either for Cyphers or the MCC sides which he led through much of the 50s and 60s. Yet in 1964, even he was moved to unstinting praise. 'Moore once again kept particularly well to Iberson...21 stumpings and 15 catches. In the gully Barnett fielded exceptionally well, taking 29 catches. Matten and Phillips were both very good in the slips and Small also was outstanding wherever he fielded. Roberts' fielding was also of a consistently high standard.'

A club newsletter entitled *Challenge* had been produced at irregular intervals since 1960 and by April 1964 had reached issue number 30. Its editor[11] had done some statistical research on the achievements of current players which deserve preservation. He listed the leading batsmen in terms of a set target of 2,000 runs in four seasons. The order was: 1 Colin Matten, 5,203 runs in 155 knocks; 2 Ted Purnell, 3,399 runs in 133; 3 Bob Phillips, 2,718 runs in 181; 4 Dick Ballam, 2,622 runs in 118; 5 Eldon Constantine, 2,250 runs in 129; 6 Ken Moore, 2,230 in 99; Bernard Seale, 2,186 runs in 105; David Stott, 2,120 runs in 85. Near misses were achieved by Alan Brooker, Wisdom, Doug Keeble, Brian Barnett, and Denis Neale. The same issue contained pen portraits of two of the First XI brightest, though occasionally flickering, stars of the 'fifties and 'sixties, Brian Barnett and Reg Collins. Barnett had topped the side's batting averages in the previous year and taken 32 wickets and 15 catches. Old Wallingtonian Collins had joined the staff of St Dunstan's after taking his degree and John Iberson introduced him to Cyphers in 1950. For Collins too, 1963 had been a fruitful year, with a stand of 151 for the 5th wicket with Neil Small against Gravesend as the highlight.

Distinguished faces of past years were still familiar at the club. Tom Jenner, retired from the headship of his school, umpired fairly regularly, as did Freddy Brigden, Jim Fleet, Jack Eastwood and Reg Hicks. But the ravages of time were beginning to take effect. Ezra Clark had been unable to play in 1964 because of illness, though his namesake Cyril had performed exceptionally well as representative of the entire Clark(e) menage; Iberson was suffering increasingly from injury to the finger joints and tendons of his left hand that had been so fiercely exercised since his school

---

[11] I believe it was Dennis Weaver, *author*.

days, resulting in the amputation of one of the extremities (the little finger joint).[12]

Matten, a seemingly indispensable force in an ageing side, decided to pursue his business career, and doubtless his cricket, in Australia. He left for the new life down under at the close of the 1964 season together with his young wife Rosemary who had been the Firsts' equally indispensable scorer for several years past. Colin Matten's last appearance on the Sunday before his departure, produced the finest innings of the season, a peerless 162 not out against Richmond.[13]

The side's strength at this time was sufficient to withstand the loss of any of its top batsmen, though the thought of losing Ibers at times of working engagement, transport mishap or attention to the tendons of his spinning fingers, caused much misgiving. As it was, his assortment of googlies and chinas, delivered with well concealed movements of shoulders, arms, hands and fingers, continued in the 1965 season to give Cyphers the edge in most of its encounters. With Small at the other end, few opponents viewed batting against Cyphers with equanimity. And the strongest of the club's local opponents, Beckenham, were by now deprived by Kent and England of their own one-man match winner, Underwood. 'Notable' scores and wicket taking carry their own messages. In batting there was only one century, Small's 105 against Streatham, but Cy Clarke as he was known to his team mates had scores of 98 against Westminster Bank, 92 against Sutton, 88 n.o. against Banstead and 66 n.o. against Beckenham.

---

[12] 1968.

[13] Colin Matten returned to England a few years later and returned to St Dunstan's as a teacher. He doesn't appear to have played again for Cyphers.

Phillips, Purnell, Barnett, Roberts and Austin all made good over-fifty contributions. In bowling it was a case of 'beat that' at either end, with a single dramatic intervention: v Westminster Bank, OR Small 9 - 26; v Dulwich, J Iberson 7-27; v Beckenham, OR Small 7-47 and 6-52; v Midland Bank, J Iberson 7-88; v Banstead, J Iberson 6-46; v Spencer, J Iberson 6-55; v Sutton, C Clarke 6-62; v MCC, J Iberson 6-66; v Barclays Bank, OR Small 5-23, J Iberson 5-54; v Midland Bank, J Iberson 5-32; v Kenley, OR Small 5-37; v O Alleynians, J Iberson 5-43. Viewed in the light of such figures, team performance seems almost too obvious for comment, though there were setbacks: P25, W12, D7, L3, Aband. 3. Batting averages in round figures were C Clarke (35), Purnell (33), Lee (26), Small (25), Barnett (24), Phillips (22). Bowling: Iberson (11), Small (11), Clarke (17), Phillips (33). The best indicator of the club's overall strength at this time is perhaps the fact that Small and Iberson were fifth and sixth respectively in the club bowling averages, with Lee (7), Matthews (10), Guest (11), and Hodges (11) above them, and Gaylarde and Cair just below in the 13s. The lower elevens' results reflected the new air of success: Second XI P24, W7, D10, L5, Aband.2; Third P24, W9, D7, L5, Aband.3; Fourth P21, W17, D3, L1; Fifth P19, W5, D3, L10, Aband. 1.

In March 1965, there was a large gathering of Cyphers and Tulse Hill Hockey members to say farewell to George Wager, the groundsman who had served the club through thick and thin, in war and peace, for 33 years. George had begun his career at the Oval under Tom Martin. When the latter was succeeded by his brother Austin in 1922, George was promoted to assistant groundsman, a job which he retained until 1932 when he moved to King's Hall Road.[14]

Club results in 1966 were the best for many a year, but once again top performers were beginning to decline and new talents were needed. And there were signs of new influences which boded ill for the game at club and every other level. But there was no obvious bowing of the head at the end of the season. Of 29 games played by the First XI, 12 were won, 5 drawn and 8 lost. Small topped the batting figures with 653 runs from 19 appearances at the wicket, twice not out, for an average of 38.47. He was followed by Phillips, Purnell and Russell. Iberson almost inevitable topped the bowling with, for him, a modest 213.3 overs, producing 60 wickets at 8.40 each. A new name appeared next, B Naylor, with an average of 14, followed by Small with 14.45, and Bob Phillips with 15.35. The Seconds went through the entire season without losing a match. P23, W9, D12, L0, Aband.2. Seale, Sweetman, Smith, Collins, Poole, Rees, and Lee, headed the averages, while in bowling Peter Smith was followed by Sweetman, Simpson, Eric Clark, Naylor, Lucas and Higgs. Other elevens kept their heads above water. The Third, P22, W8, L4, D7, Aband.3; Fourth, P23, W6, D5, L9, Aband.3; Fifth, P15, W4, D3, L6, Aband.2. Sunday results were much in line.

Cricket Week in 1966, the year of the club's 75th anniversary, brought a new all-rounder and batting strengths into prominence. Bob Phillips scored the dreaded 99 in a victorious engagement with Winchmore Hill, and went on to claim 7 for 33 with his leg and off cutters, and Chris Russell, another stylish bat with plenty of representative cricket to look forward to, scored 61 against

---

[14] *Kentish Times*, 5 March 1965

Midland Bank. Rain washed out much of the week, but two other Cyphers characters worthy of special mention played between downpours. Dennis Weaver, a bowler whose somewhat leisurely action belied a penetrating performance, took 5 for 34 in a losing encounter with Canterbury St Lawrence; his faithful support of the club over many years included the editorship of a newsletter and the presentation of an annual award for team performance. And Doug Keeble, a large man in every way, devoted to music, beer and cricket to a degree which forbids any order of priority, made a typically grafted 32 in the Midland Bank match.

Coincidence, always to be sought in a game so infused with statistics, was seen by the local press[15] to mark also the 75th birthday of Rupert Holloway. That the club's longest serving player, captain, chairman and president was born in the year of the club's inauguration had so far escaped public notice.

It was also the year in which long incubating disputes in the club game festered in open debate. It was the year in which the great game itself seemed to approach irresistibly a series of watersheds; of political intervention over South Africa, of the 'bouncer' controversy which was acerbated by Underwood being felled by a short ball from Griffith, of crowd misbehaviour in the West Indies, and of discontent among top players in the higher reaches of a game that saw itself as the poor relation of the sporting world. The Don had played his last game, Hobbs, 'Titch' Freeman and Hammond had died within two years of each other. As Ming potters said when they produced a bad piece, God's finger was pointing the wrong way.

---

[15] *Kentish Times*, 15 April/ 29 July 1966

Club cricket, too, was at the crossroads, with newspaper headlines promising a split between north and south London clubs[16]. No wonder that Cyphers had begun, literally and metaphorically, to burn. Its pride and joy, the pavilion that many referred to as 'the barn' and thought too grand, too big or too impersonal, suffered four disastrous fires[17]. The dinner dance at which they celebrated the club's 75th birthday had to be held at the Greyhound Hotel, Croydon, and Rupert Holloway, responding to the toast of 'The President' proposed by chairman Bernard Newton, took the opportunity to lament the passing of a once prosperous social scene at King's Hall Road, and to remember nostalgically how in times gone by they had danced late into the night in front of the pavilion.

Time and money seemed to be running out and nobody quite knew how to stop the rot.

---

[16] *Evening News*, 4 December 1966

[17] There was a police investigation but no charges were preferred. The teenage bar steward resigned after a fourth attempt to burn down the pavilion.

6

The League and Farewell!

The controversy hinted at in earlier chapters came to a head in November 1966 and led to a series of articles in the London *Evening News* which named the chief participants of a squabble within club cricket's own corridors.

That newspaper's headline on Tuesday 29 November 1966, read: 'E.M. Wellings Slams Surrey League Scheme' and under that banner heading it punned 'A Subba row in cricket'. To an extent it was all good slapstick comedy, with a big name to play with in Subba Row, and an opportunity for Lord Rothermere's chief evening newspaper to fire its lesser guns at Lord Beaverbrook's evening flagship the *Evening Standard*, which for more than ten years had sponsored the popular and widely supported London Club League with its North and South tables of merit. For those who were devoted to a game which had become a vital aspect of social life in towns and villages the length and breadth of Britain in the course of some 200 years, it was much more.

'Sixteen clubs have toed the line laid down by Subba Row of the Old Whitgiftians, and decided to form a league, starting in 1968, under the high sounding title Surrey Cricket Clubs Championship Association', ran the introduction to Wellings' article. It went on:

> How firm their purpose will prove if the leaders of the group fail to have the rules of the Club Cricket Conference amended at the March meeting, remains to be seen... Such a drastic change cannot safely be entrusted to a handful of Gunpowder Plotters. It should be worked out inside London Club Cricket's governing body. Some of the sixteen have entered not so much because they want competitive club cricket, but because they fear to be left out and so risk losing fixtures...

It all seemed a trifle melodramatic at the time, but the last point was a valid indication of serious rifts within the Conference.

Ted Purnell and Raman Subba Row had enjoyed a long and harmonious relationship as skippers of two sides that had played each other in friendly rivalry for many years; and Cyphers' captain was among the first to be consulted by the man who had won so much respect as England's, Northampton's, and OW's opener. After the event, Purnell would acknowledge his friend's solemn warning that if Cyphers stayed outside the Surrey League plan, they would inevitably lose some of their longest standing and most important fixtures and that their very existence would be threatened. But he, Purnell, was the emissary of a club that was implacably opposed to the league concept and had made up its mind to steer clear of any such proposals. Clubs such as Cyphers and Old Whitgiftians – to which might be added names like Beddington and Banstead, Beckenham and Gravesend, Spencer and Dulwich – needed no points incentive to sharpen their traditional rivalries. They had played each other decade after decade, season after season, to win and, if winning proved beyond them, then to hold on with grim determination for the draw. And there was the rub. League cricket was all about winning. About maximum points, and with such criterion go all kinds of unspoken but clearly foreseen nuances of attitude, on and off the field. In a sense, club cricket was undergoing the same metamorphosis as the first-class game, suffering from comparison with Australian and West Indies performances, responding almost in the dark to the challenges of a fast changing and inflationary world, to television, to demands for sporting excellence from classroom to Olympic stadium, for more money at every level to ensure continuity and player loyalty. It was, at the moment, an evolutionary process but everyone involved knew how easily it could become revolutionary.

When the *Evening News* returned to the subject in February 1967 it headed its report, 'CCC Warns League Cricketers':

> Member clubs of the Club Cricket Conference will not be allowed to play league cricket. The 17 in the newly formed Surrey championship, due to start in 1968, face expulsion from the C.C.C... Major Woods, the Conference Secretary, stated today that the Executive Council has ruled that their championship contravenes the rules and that the Council does not propose to amend the pertinent rule which forbids such competitive play...

The clubs named in the report as the seventeen who proposed to go it alone, made unhappy reading for those who would be left to play under Conference terms — Addiscombe, Banstead, Beddington, Cheam, Dulwich, East Molesey, Epsom, Guildford, Malden Wanderers, Mitcham, Old Emmanuel, Old Whitgiftians, Purley, Spencer, Streatham, Sunbury and Sutton. There were, admittedly, some notable abstentions; but there were ominous suggestions that it would not be long before senior Kent clubs took a lead from Surrey and formed themselves into a protective coterie. Raman Subba Row warned Ted Purnell in the friendliest way that delay might leave Cyphers and other clubs of similar stature dangerously exposed in a sporting no-man's land. Given a Kent league, Cyphers would have to make do with the opposition that remained, and inevitably it would in the end be forced to take its place in a grouping that was not of its own choice or making.[1]

For the moment, the traditional fixture list remained intact and a season of goodwill, at least on the surface, beckoned in 1967. Indeed, in April there was a reminder of another secure period of club cricket, the 1930s, that was to be shattered by unexpected events. It came in the shape of an invitation to Whizz from JAC Benthall the Beckenham Cricket Chairman, to the opening of that club's new pavilion. It read:

Dear Mr Wisdom

You will recall that you were in the Cyphers side that played on the day your new pavilion was opened in 1936. You may also recall that your opponents that day were Beckenham.

---

[1] I have paraphrased the account given to me by Ted Purnell at the end of his playing days. Although he regretted the decicion in retrospect, he was at the time implacably opposed to the league idea, but pointed out that he negotiated as club captain whose hands were tied whether or not he approved. *Author.*

> Now, 31 years later, we are opening our new pavilion on a day (29th April) that Cyphers are our opponents. We are therefore attempting to gather together as many of both sides that played in the 1936 match as we are able. Dick Moreland (who himself played and who is now our president) and I sincerely hope that you can take wine with us at 12.30 pm and lunch at 1.30 pm.

By July, there was no sign of a setting sun. 'Cyphers win 7 out of 8' said a local paper headline[2]. The report stated 'Cyphers, one of the largest private cricket clubs in the C.C.C. recorded their ninth successive win by beating Dulwich on Saturday. In fact, Cyphers won seven out of eight week-end fixtures, and drew the other.' In six out of eight games that first week-end in July, the opposition was dismissed for less than a hundred. And the most impressive performances came from lower elevens, with the new boy B McKeough taking 8 for 32 for Gaylarde's Fifth XI against Lensbury, Alan Scott scoring a resolute 46 n.o. for the 2nd XI, Wisdom now with the 4th XI making a match saving 36 n.o., Chris Poole and Russell making 64 and 32 respectively for the Sunday 'B', and Ballam registering 99 for the Sunday 'C'. By the end of the season, statistics were not quite so rosy, but they showed a creditable picture overall, with the First XI having won 10, drawn 8 and lost 2 of the 20 matches played, with 1 abandoned.

The skipper's praise of his side's batting in his end-of-season report was, by his conservative standard, almost unqualified. 'Our batting was the most reliable in depth for many seasons, probably since the war. Not only was it reliable, runs were scored, at least on hard wickets, at about 85 an hour, thus giving us the

---

[2] *Kentish Times*, Friday 7 July, 1967.

opportunity for an early declaration, or more time to bowl the opposition out.' There was praise too for the opening attack of Small and Phillips, and for the magnificent intervention of off spinner MA Sweetman who took his opportunity when Iberson was forced to have surgical treatment for a damaged finger and was out of action until late July. Sweetman took 41 wickets at 12.8 runs apiece, while Iberson – with a forced change of action caused by the loss of a finger joint – produced the remarkable figures of 40 wickets in eight games, at an average of under 10. CJ Russell headed the First eleven batting averages at 40.1, closely followed by Small at 39.8; then came Bob Phillips and Colin Matten with 35.3 and 33.3 respectively. The First XI was also graced by a second Phillips at this time, Bob's brother John, who had scored runs consistently in all sides from the Fifth up, and who ended the season fifth in the senior side's batting averages at 26.1. Of the century makers, Russell had made 135 against Winchmore Hill and 120 against Malden Wanderers; and Small 100 against Westminster Bank. On the bowling front the figures were more decisive. Iberson (9.4), Sweetman (12.8), Phillips RC (17.8), Small (18.7). But Small, by a considerable distance the fastest bowler on the Southern club scene at this time, bowled 255 overs against his nearest rival's (Sweetman) 185.

The club's leading batting figures (excepting those already given, were: Keeble D (42.4), Roberts J (33.0), Winstone HVF (29.8), Smith PB (28.1), Seale B (24.5), Purnell EG (24.5), Murray G (24.2), Scott A (23.6), Letchford J (23.5), Letchford K (22.8), Wisdom E (21.4), Noakes J (20.3).[3]

---

[3] Figures include Cricket Week, evening and Sunday fixtures.

Warning signals came early in 1968 to demonstrate that the crisis in cricket was by no means confined to the lesser mortals of the club game. In the West Indies the crowd intervened with bottles and sticks to bring play to a halt when the home side headed for defeat and Butcher was out to a catch that the crowd decided had been grounded by Parks. Not even the word of Sobers, who was batting with Butcher, mollified the faithful. Players' dressing rooms were filled with the 'tear' gas used by police to gain control. 'NOW CAGE IN TEST HOOLIGANS' demanded the *Daily Express*. The troubles of club cricket seemed, for the moment at least, to fade into insignificance compared to those of the senior practitioners of the game.

The end of an era may have beckoned for clubs like Cyphers, but familiar names, faces and places were still paramount for those who simply got on with the serious business of week-end cricket. Or more exactly, perhaps, got on with the enjoyment of friendly encounter — and never so much as in the popular Cyphers tour of Sussex.

Memories of much that happened on the King's Hall Road ground may have faded over the years, but the Sussex Tour is evergreen in the minds of those who went on it. David Stott, for example, had been at the club from the golden year of 1952 until 1956 before he went on his first sojourn, and teamed up with stalwarts of the circus like Peter Bavister and Colin Mote who each swore that they would make a century and achieved it by the Thursday evening: one hundred Mackeson stouts apiece! Forty years on he recalled the match against Steyning skippered by Eric Wadman in which a young Sussex hopeful hit everything on the off side and usually out of sight; until Wadman put himself on to bowl with well contrived line and every fielder on the off, and the

would surely be close to the head of the table however it was presented, wasn't pacified but he was outvoted.

In 1967, the old mathematical practice was resumed with an apologia attached which read: 'These Averages...are not to be used as proof of merit or non-merit of individual players...'. Perhaps the heading of the covering note spoke most eloquently 'Adult Reading Only!' If nothing else, the document provides a convenient way of looking at the club's membership, and at the waxing and waning strengths that were to see it through to its last decade of independent existence.

õ

By 1969, playing membership was at an all-time high. Performance through the elevens was patchy, but by and large it looked healthy enough, with 72 matches won, 42 lost and 47 drawn of the 161 played, allowing for cancelled and abandoned games.

BATTING AVERAGES 1969 (limited to 10 completed innings:

	Ave
Russell, CJ	38.9
Duncan,	36.0
Saward. D	32.3
Phillips, RC	30.9
Poole, CJ	30.6
Smith, PB	28.0

Russell, P	26.9
Seale, BH	26.6
Baker, N	25.2
Waite, R	24.0
Ford, C	23.8
Constantine, ES	23.3
Neill, TV	22.9
Tomkins, HJ	22.5
Rees, P	21.9
Scott, AL	21.7
Florence, WA	21.2
Richards, DJ	20.8
Murray, GC	19.7
Smith, HA	19.2
Phillips, JH	19.1
Letchford, K	18.2
Roberts, J	18.0
Purnell, EG	17.9
Lee, GS	17.8
Kelsh, NJ	17.5
Collins, RW	17.0
Keeble, DJL	16.7
Goward, R	15.5
Gandy, BM	15.4
Weaver, K	15.3
Ishthikar, M	15.2
Simmons	14.2
Mitchell, S	14.1
Wisdom, EM	14.0
Champion, RAH	13.6

Abbott, P	13.5
Tomkins, J	13.4
Wentworth, D	13.2
Barnett, BA	13.0
Cair, J	12.9
Sweetman, MA	12.6
Neale, DM	12.5
Letchford, J	12.4
Russell, W	11.7
Brooker, AF	11.5
Simpson, JA	11.2
Batterbee, C	10.9
James, G	10.6
Phillips, Roger	10.3
Higgs, G	10.2
Howe, J	10.1
Trinchero, D	10.0

Bowling averages help to supplement this record of playing members at the close of the 'Sixties.

	Ave
Brown, J	5.1
White, J	8.4
Letchford, J	9.8
Ishthtikar, M	10.7
Iberson, J	11.8
McKeough, B	12.4
Guest, J	12.6
Cair, JN	12.8

Neill, TV	12.9
Stevens, A	13.4
Letchford, K	13.5
Mitchell, S	14.3
Russell, CJ	14.5
Cooper, B	15.0
Waite, R	15.1
Weaver, D	15.2
Simpson, JA	15.3
Rhodes, L	15.6
Davie, ACG	15.7
Phillips, RC	16.0
Higgs, G	16.5
Thomas, P	16.6
Barnett, B	16.7
Lucas, A	17.2
Weaver, K	17.5
Gaylarde, WW	18.0
White, G	18.1
Smith, AF	18.4
Hodges, TR	19.2
James, G	19.6
Murray, GC	19.8
Sweetman, MA	19.9
Gates, MJ	22.8
Phillips, JH	23.1
Lee, GS	25.1
Purnell, EG	33.3

Looking at the figures, unconvincing as statistics can be, leads inevitably to the thought that the end of an era approached. Small, so recently the terror of club batsmen in the South, had begun to suffer the aches and pains that are the fast bowler's lot and his familiar name had disappeared from the playing lists, though he continued to play the occasional game elsewhere. Purnell, who had once led the club bowling and batting tables, was now at the foot of the former, and half way down the latter. It was time for that exceptional sportsman to relinquish the captaincy he had held with distinction for more than a decade, through some of the club's finest moments.

Ted Purnell is one of the select band of Cyphers players who stand out from the general run; *sui generis* as it were. Like Rupert Holloway before him, he had been an outstanding footballer as well as cricketer, playing for Corinthian Casuals before cricket took over completely. His long sojourn with the MCC made him a familiar figure at the Oval and HQ, and county players and administrators held him in high regard as an elegant bat, excellent close fielder, capable bowler and a captain who commanded instant respect. In fact, he was a 'natural' at almost any ball game. Yet, almost impossible though it is for many who played with him to believe, he suffered all his life from epilepsy, and at the end of his playing days experienced a massive cerebral attack, though he recovered from it and mercifully retained his memory, which embraced an encyclopaedic knowledge of cricket, past and present. Speaking to him, one had the impression that he could recite *Wisden* word for word from the inception of that publication. Characteristically, he marked the end of his serious playing career (he went on as an occasional player and temporary skipper until 1974) by taking the Colts under his wing and spending every available moment with them in the nets at the ground and indoors at Crystal Palace. His contribution to Cyphers Club was extraordinary and unique, though he would have been the first to insist that others such as Simmons, Webb, Holloway, Jennings and Wardle, the fleeting Johnston, Wisdom, Kelsh and, more recently, Iberson and Small, were the true stars in that minor Kentish firmament.

Bob Phillips took over the Captaincy for the 1969 season and he was to skipper the Club through a period of growing financial strain and membership decline to the verge of its reluctant league debut.

Results in the years from 1970 to 1973 showed a playing picture that was largely in tune with the depressive mood at what had become something of a last-chance saloon at King's Hall Road. From 72 won, 42 lost, 47 drawn in 1969, it was 52 won, 58 lost and 44 drawn in 1970; then 45 won 53 lost, 55 drawn in 1971; a sudden resurgence in 1972 with 67 won, 49 lost and 50 drawn; and the nadir of 1973, 39 won, 51 lost, 42 drawn.

Perhaps the most hopeful sign at this juncture was the successful entry of young members of families who had long been part of the club's tradition and history. Denis Neale – whose Third XI vied with Gaylarde's Fifth for renown which had as much to do with hospitality as with cricket – had been split in his loyalties by the need to keep wicket for the Seconds and even the First in recent times. Now his son Guy was showing off a family talent behind the stumps with 15 catches and 6 stumpings, putting him at second place in the club's overall 'dismissals' table and overtaking by some distance his father's mere six stumpings and no catches. The boy's batting showed promise too.

Another Duncan, H, had joined the long line of forebears who had been part of the Cyphers family since its inception in the earliest years of the century. Indeed, a team made up entirely of Duncans, as well as a Syme & Duncan XI, challenged club sides from time to time. The latest of that line, a promising keeper, was embroiled in the fierce competition at the time for a place behind the stumps, ending the season just behind Bob Jones (now 2nd and occasionally 3rd XI keeper) with 12 catches and 6 stumpings. Wentworth headed that table with 13 catches and 11 removals of the bails.

There was another family reinforcement in the shape of John Letchford, whose older brother Keith was a well established member of the First and, in the tradition of some of the best Cyphers players, a 'Stoic'. Their father, Wally, was a doyen of the post Second World War years whose all-round feats were crowned in 1955 with the remarkable figures of 7 for 9 against Private Banks IV.

But if that other perennial, Purnell, had decided to stay with the club to the bitter end, Iberson, without question its most distinguished player over almost twenty years, decided to call it a day. In fact, he played his last game for the club in 1969, when, as was almost written in stone, he headed the First eleven bowling table.

It is always invidious to highlight individuals in what is essentially a team game, and certainly John Iberson himself would have none of it. But his record, not just as a cricketer but as an amusing, highly intelligent cavalier among his fellow men, cannot be gainsaid. With John there is an endless store of anecdote, yet paradoxically, it is the statistics he so despised that remain as proof of his place in the game he loved.

David Roberts in an article on Cyphers[5] wrote: 'His subject at St Dunstan's is Economics and there has been a sufficient supply of batsmen to meet his demand'. He invited the reader to glance at the bare statistics.

> For Cyphers 1841 wickets for 18238 runs, ave 9.9
> For Stoics 258 wickets for 2614 runs, ave 10.1
> For Casuals 172 wickets for 1654 runs, ave 9.6
> For Hertfordshire 201 wickets for 2701 runs, ave 13.4
> Total 2472 wickets for 25207 runs, ave 10.2

In Mendelsohn's Centenary history *Stoics Cricket Club 1877 – 1977*, Iberson dominates the notable performances pages from 1954 onward. Versus Old Hurstjohnians, 7 – 30; v Eastern Command, 7 – 13. 1955 v Guildford, 7 – 71. His apparent devotion to the numeral 7 was overcome in the match with Eastbourne in 1955, 6 – 36. 1956 v Old Cholmelians, 6 – 26; v Old Hurstjohnians 8 – 44; v Ditchling 6 – 31.

The last word on a subject that inevitably features heavily in any history of the Cyphers must go to that most remarkable of club cricketers, Jack Hyams, himself 76 years of age in 1997, with nearly 120,000 runs under his belt and still playing for Brondesbury in the Middlesex County League and for Cheshunt in the Hertfordshire League. When he was told that this book was being produced he wrote to the author:

> I did play against Cyphers CC for Finchley in 1978. Keith
> Letchford was in that Cyphers eleven, and as you may know he is
> the fixtures secretary of the Stoics CC, for which I have been a

---

[5] *Cricketer*, Vol 1 No 19, 1976.

playing member for 35 years and am still a vice-president. Whilst on the subject of the Stoics, it is through them that I played with both Neill Small and John Iberson. In fact, whilst on the Cambridge College tour of 1963 I shared a room with John for the first two days (I could only do 2 days of the 5). On the first day I was successful with the bat and he with the ball. The next day after having kept me awake practically all night talking about cricket, and prancing round the bedroom in his pyjamas demonstrating his different types of googly, he finally flopped asleep. The next morning, bleary eyed (a mixture of drink and lack of sleep) he turned up for the match late (as usual) and informed the skipper Gerald Plumbly that he was in no condition to play and would rather help with the scoring!! Gerald however would have none of this and insisted that he bowled, and of course he bowled beautifully. After this game I had to leave, but John completed the whole tour and on the last three days took 4 - 64, 3 - 62, 3 - 35. The last time I saw him was roughly 10 years ago when I was playing for the Stoics against Old Dunstonians and he came along in the evening and was pleased to see me and surprised that I was still playing for the Stoics...

It should be added as a footnote to Cyphers' signal contribution to the Stoics that Bob Phillips in 1969 joined the very select list of those who have scored two centuries or more for the club. He registered 119 against Jesus College, Cambridge, and 105 not out against Sunbury.

Others who were in their different ways as much part of the Cyphers scene as Purnell, Iberson and Small, carried on to the end. It is not possible to name them all, but two remain in the memory as 'characters' and devoted club players; HJ (Tommy) Tomkins and WW (Bill) Gaylarde. Both have featured prominently in our story, yet a few more words need to be written. Of Tomkins senior, it has to be said that he was a man of the most extreme modesty in the very important job he undertook in life as a senior official of the Bank of England. He was one of the world's most distinguished experts in the planning and organisation of fiscal systems. When, in the aftermath of war, new nation states were created, it was the knowledgeable Mr Tomkins who was sent to organise their monetary wherewithal, the printing and minting and distribution of notes and coins. It is a fair bet that he sat among statesmen, economists and financiers much as he sat among cricketers in committee, rolling his own cigarettes, chain smoking and, when so inclined, being quietly bloody minded. But his priorities were always absolute and it was an important matter of international finance indeed that, in later days, kept him away from an appointment with Cyphers Fourth or Fifth at weekends. He would arrive from Africa or the Americas or the Far East on a Saturday morning, replete with his well-worn and carefully packed bag, to turn out for whichever side required him, as if he had never been away, and be off again on Monday, on aircraft that still boasted propellers. He was a steady, correct and steadfast batsman, capable of grafting good scores in often dire circumstances. When he skippered a side, he was also capable of sending prospective members of his team their batting and fielding positions on selection cards posted on the previous Wednesday. And while he would seldom proffer an opinion on the monetary matters which were at his fingertips and were of burning interest to most of mankind, he would give an adamant opinion on any cricket matter at the drop of a hat and would seldom brook contradiction. He was, like most club players, a modest cricketer, yet to him nothing was ever quite on the same scale of importance, or as close to cataclysm, as a dropped catch or being bowled through the gate. Being out was for him a matter for prolonged mourning. By the early 'Seventies his son John was proceeding with more equanimity along a well worn trail at King's Hall Road – St Dunstan's school, Cyphers 5th XI under Gaylarde's aegis, and thus through the sides to the First XI where he became established as a fluent bat and an excellent fielder.

As for Bill Gaylarde, he was, despite his eccentricities, a man made for the rough and tumble of the competitive game, and even in his seventies was still high in the club's bowling averages; so good in fact at putting his ordinary looking off-breaks on a sixpence, despite the majestic effort of turning his arm over, that he was sometimes called on to play for the Second XI, and all was well so long as the captain remembered to put him at old-fashioned long stop in his field placing. To the very end, his peremptory manner needed to be explained to opposing batsmen and skippers who were unaware of his reputation. It has been said that no man knows the true meaning of fear who has not accepted a lift from Gaylarde late in the evening after a riotous session in the club bar (before the drink and drive laws, that is). To be in the passenger seat when Bill reversed onto a main highway without even glancing at a side or rear view mirror, in a car laden to the gunwales with the impedimenta of his trade, is something that only the very bravest ever aspired to. He must surely have been the most Quixotic of Cliftonians, old and new.

Perhaps the transition from club cricket as it was to league cricket as it became, is best summed up in a small essay by a Cyphers player who became a noted sports commentator, Rob Bonnet:

> And so my first season was in 1970... Sundays only until mid-July since I was still playing at school, but then in the holidays I scraped

into the first eleven that - I suspect - is still talked about as the last Cyphers 'dream team'. Purnell, Iberson, Banks and the Phillips brothers in - I think - their last full season at the club, with the nostalgic talk in the bar of Neill Small still relatively fresh. I was part of the dreamy soft-underbelly, making up the numbers and usually sulking after being taken off after a fiery spell of 1 for 45...This, in fairness, was a strong side which led the inaugural season of the South Thames League well into the summer, largely through the batting of Bob Phillips and the bowling of Brian Banks on a wicket once disparagingly described by Nick Cosh (Surrey, Cambridge University and Old Alleynians) as a *******
beach...[6]

In 1973 there was a dummy run for the club in the relentless surge of league cricket. On 26 May of that year Cyphers First and Second elevens played Lloyds Bank home and away under the new rules of the already established South Thames Cricket League and won both games handsomely. Ted Purnell scored 101 not out for the senior side and the South Thames League *Bulletin* remarked: 'The many cricketers who have admired Purnell's stalwart services in Cyphers' cause will be delighted at his latest achievement'.

1974 saw the club's first full season of South Thames League cricket, the senior side occupying ninth place in the end-of-season table, the Second XI third from bottom at thirteenth place. The First XI table shows both the new fixture list and the method of establishing precedence. M=most runs, L=least runs, B=bonus points:

---

[6] Note to author.

	P	W	M	L	B	P
Forest Hill	14	10	2	0	6	96
Bexley	14	9	1	1	8	69
Kenley	14	7	0	1	8	69
Nat West Bank	14	7	1	0	8	69
Midland Bank	14	6	1	1	2	61
Frindsbury	14	5	2	1	4	59
Sidcup	14	5	2	0	5	59
Catford Wanderers	14	3	3	1	3	44
CYPHERS	14	4	0	2	5	41
Old Alleynians	14	3	2	2	3	41
Bexleyheath	14	3	0	5	6	39
Alleyn OB	14	3	1	0	3	35
Britannic House	14	2	2	2	3	35
Lloyds Bank	14	3	1	0	3	35
Bickley Park	14	1	1	3	1	20

Batting and bowling lists provide a glimpse of the last generation of Cyphers men to play on the turf that had in its time been host to the likes of WG and Murdoch, Beldam, Gillingham and Robins, May and Laker, Subba Row and the delightful West Indian Dr Bertie Clarke, and many another cricketer of first class and club renown. Figures are irrelevant. The names in the first season of the league were: Murray, G, Lee, G, Thomson, K, Bangay, C, Florence, W, Saward, D, Banks, B, Letchford, K, Roberts, J, Bonnet, R, Smith, A, Purnell, E, Waite, R, Wentworth, D, White, G, Scott, A, Tomkins, J, Davey, A, James, G, Barnett, B, Pannett, J. They were soon joined by Perera, C, Pichowski, N, Randeneyi, S, Cook, C. A few more names should be added, players who in the past or succeeding years occupied places higher up: Abbott, P,

Brooker, A, Jones, R, Higgs, G, Ishthikar, M, Phillips, R, Seale, B, Linford, D, Best, R, Sealy, G, Trinchero, D, Lucas, A, Poole, C, Gaylarde, WW, Cair, J, Champion, R, Faulkner, A, Wiseman, D, Sharland, A, Askew, A, Weaver, JK, McCormack, P, Stevens, A, Turner, C, Lawrence, P, Tomkins, HJ, Keeble, D, Knight, D, Duncan, JW, Duncan, W, Duncan, H, Duncan, R, Ohlson, J, Charlesworth, R, Runcorn, N, Nichols, P, Leigh, E, Asquith, Robert, Asquith, Richard, Harris, B, Heed, E, Aston, M, Recontre, A, Glazebrook, P, Milner, J, Hector, E, Haydon, R, Brown, D, Neale, C, Laker, J (as distinct from JC), Hector, E, Hamil, J, Gooding, O. That, in the main, was the playing membership that took the club into the new era. President at this time was William 'Bill' Russell, wicket keeper and voluntary groundsman. Chairman was Tommy Tomkins, Secretary David Brown, Treasurer Tony Stevens.

Jim Roberts had taken over the club captaincy from Bob Phillips in 1973 but in 1975 he wanted to relinquish the job and Ted Purnell offered reluctantly to take on the job until a younger and more permanent skipper could be found. Thus Ted took charge during two of the early years of the league combat he had so steadfastly resisted, 1975 and 1976, and he talked his friend John Iberson into a temporary return. The latter topped the bowling averages for both seasons, with figures of 14.0 and 12.65, but neither his bowling nor Purnell's batting was any longer up to the cut and thrust of weekly competition, and the side's position in the middle of the table hardly changed. The Second XI however sank to the penultimate place in its table in both years. Keith Letchford took over the captaincy in 1977, to be succeeded by Dick Waite in 1980. Then came Ken Slater in 1981, Jim Roberts in '83, Keith Letchford again in '84. The days of seemingly endless periods of settled leadership, of Simmons and Holloway, Wisdom and Purnell at the helm, had gone for ever.

In its last gasp as a traditional club, standing aside from the hurly burly of the league game, Cyphers had seen most of its major fixtures disappear, as Raman Subba Row had warned when the idea was first rejected. The Kent and Surrey leagues had taken away Beddington and Banstead, Beckenham and Whitgiftians and some of the major banks. In the end, the club's belated entry into the South Thames League became its only way to retain any kind of fixture list. With senior players leaving or at the end of their careers, a reduced membership and consequently reduced match fees and subs, diminishing bar takings (and the inevitable 'fruit' machine) the only real source of income, and ever increasing costs of ground maintenance, rent and rates, the time had come for drastic measures.

It was for Denis Neale, schoolmaster, all-rounder and practised negotiator, to take up the cudgels in a last effort to save the ailing club. He was well placed to devote himself to an almost insoluble problem since a back injury had brought his captaincy of the Thirds and thus his playing days to an abrupt end. Seeking to salvage the sinking club that he had been part of since the 'Fifties was a task that would occupy him for years to come and he took it on with every expectation of success. But some things are beyond mortal aid. In the case of ailing sports clubs foundering in unfavourable economic waters there is usually the certainty of death from a collective lemming instinct.

Imminent collapse was widely predicted and, as usually happens at such moments, the membership was held in a vice-like grip of nostalgia and ennui. Meetings of all the sections, cricket, tennis and bowls, were held jointly and severally to try to find a way forward, a route to salvation; and at every turn the membership was agreed only upon one thing, that it did not want change. The bar, except on match nights – and often they were no exception – was empty but for a few ageing stalwarts who really rather resented intrusion into that small corner of England they had made their own. There was always an argument in favour of leaving things as they were, a comfortable reminder of times gone by. The ground, and in particular the tennis courts, deteriorated badly. Ground committees with voluntary helpers tried to take the place of experienced ground staff. A fishing club was among the many ingenious money-raising ploys. It lasted for some three or four years under the aegis of the bar steward, Doug Jordan.

The set up was complex. King's Hall Sports Ground were the owners of the ground and all the property, and the shares which had been allocated to the founding members had now passed into the hands of a fourth or fifth generation of their successors. Cyphers was the tenant or licensee of KHSG, and its three sections, cricket, tennis and bowls, contributing proportionately to make up the annual rent. Cyphers' Executive, made up of HJ 'Tommy' Tomkins (cricket), Warwick Booth (tennis), Bill Parker (Bowls), Arthur Bucksey as bar committee chairman, and Denis Neale as chairman, turned for its salvation to the ultimate power, King's Hall Sports Ground Ltd, who suggested that an attempt should be made to find a commercial organisation that would be able to take on the lease which KHSG had granted to Cyphers, while allowing the club to retain its facilities. The national press began to take an interest and a number of insurance companies, some with contacts with club members, came forward in response to stories of possible closure. In particular, two large firms of brokers showed an interest, Price Forbes and Sedgwick Collins, who had to hire pitches for their employees to play on. Slowly, an arrangement was arrived at whereby Price Forbes and Sedgwick Collins jointly took over the lease of the ground and pavilion from KHSG and Cyphers Club became, in effect, a licensee of the two broking firms, at an agreed and plausible rent. To all appearances, it was an ideal arrangement. Some of the old players and the brokers' directors were old friends.

In the first few years of the arrangement, while the club adapted to the rigours of the league game, the directors on both sides went along in tandem and conspicuous harmony. John Breething, a director of Sedgwicks and subsequently chairman of Holmsdale Cricket Club in Sevenoaks, was responsible for the management of the King's Hall Road ground and he seemed to understand Cyphers' problems and aims. But such arrangements always contain the seeds of disaster. Sedgwick Collins and Price Forbes merged and became Sedgwick Forbes with new directors and a different outlook on life. Old pledges of fraternity, to be solemnised in the bar on summer evenings after hard-fought cricket matches, gave way to the reality of a few office workers dressed in grey trousers and black shoes playing a version of cricket that was decidedly foreign to the front wicket at King's Hall Road, and to an empty, forlorn bar. Tulse Hill Hockey Club, a valuable and prestigious tenant, left to share Honor Oak's ground. The new owners wanted King's Hall Road for football in winter.

The slow progression into total dependence was predictable. Sedgwick Forbes as it now was took over the entire responsibility for the project, put in their own manager, and Cyphers simply paid a rent for its facilities, part in cash, part in 'rental labour' in the shape of Bill Russell as ground manager, Arthur Bucksey as bar manager and Warwick Booth as tennis organiser, though the state of the once proud championship courts suggested that the demise of that section could not be long delayed.

The Bowls section, unhappy about the entire arrangement, decided to pull out from the Cyphers triumvirate and made its own terms with the new owners. In the end, only Cyphers cricket remained to negotiate an existence based on the goodwill of the owners, and goodwill is a notoriously frail ally in any business deal. In 1979, Sedgwicks demanded £1000 per tennis court for upkeep and so tennis ceased. In 1981, Cyphers members were refused permission to use the clubhouse bar from Monday to Friday. Committee meetings were held at members' homes. A new board of directors was eventually elected and in 1983 a grandiose scheme to sell the main clubhouse and ground to Sedgwicks and retain the back pitch with a new, small pavilion was floated. Before it could come into effect, however, the new plan was overtaken by discussions which gave rise to the amalgamation of Catford and Cyphers Cricket Clubs.

That alliance came about in 1985. The cypher and the prancing horse of Kent were joined by Catford's familiar tree in the new emblem of Catford Cyphers Cricket Club. The merger was negotiated on Cyphers' side by Tommy Tomkins, Tony Stevens and Bill Florence, and they became the advance guard of the move to Rubens Street, Catford.[7] Howard Beardwell, whose very name

---

[7] Denis Neale provided much of this 'winding up' information in a letter to the author of 30 Dec 1997. His note concludes: 'After the ground and pavilion were sold and the company went into voluntary liquidation, some money was available to help the new formed joint club...the final vestige of Cyphers CC is the Cyphers CC Trust Fund, the trustees of which are Howard Beardwell and

was part of Cyphers' identity, became joint president with John Clegg of the newly constituted club.

Bill Florence took on the captaincy of the side from its rebirth and, after the expected pangs of birth, he began to see a return for his pains. He relinquished the job to a Catford man in 1987. The new club rose steadily in the South Thames League, and kept its head above water in new and more modest seas. May it be remembered well.

myself". It is that fund which makes possible the printing of this brief history.
HVFW

Notes